Reel Histories:
Studies in American Film

Reel Histories:
Studies in American Film

Edited by Melissa Croteau

PRESS
AMERICANA

Hollywood • Los Angeles
2008

Press Americana
The Press of Americana: The Institute for the Study of American Popular Culture
7095 Hollywood Boulevard, 1240, Hollywood, California 90028-8903
http://www.americanpopularculture.com

Library of Congress Cataloging-in-Publication Data

Reel histories : studies in American film / edited by Melissa Croteau.
p. cm.
ISBN 978-0-9789041-5-9
1. Motion pictures--United States--History. 2. Motion pictures--Social aspects--
United States. I. Croteau, Melissa.
PN1993.5.U6R442 2008
791.430973--dc22
2008000547

TABLE OF CONTENTS

INTRODUCTION

The Dialectics of American Film:
Points of Resistance and Acceptance

Melissa Croteau

> In the study of popular culture, we should always start here: with the double-stake in popular culture, the double movement of containment and resistance, which is always inevitably inside it.
>
> -Stuart Hall

Movies entertain, enrage, and intrigue us. We shape them and, in turn, are shaped by them. If cultural studies has taught us anything, it is that all texts are ideological and must be read as artifacts that blossomed in a particular place and time, within a specific culture, and for more or less discernable reasons. Interrogating the agendas of such cultural products has become one of the primary tasks of scholars of film and media. Formalist close readings of individual films, as elegant as those analyses may be, are no longer viable in the academic arena because we have recognized that by deconstructing the complexity of intersecting socio-cultural and historical contexts in the movies we produce, we can effectively anatomize the dominant ideologies that pervade and often control our lives as well as our own worldviews. As the unexamined life may not be worth living, so the unexamined film may not be worth believing, but viewers do seem to absorb – consciously or unconsciously – the ideologies marketed to them via myriad media outlets.

In the past few decades, film studies has embraced the cultural studies methodologies, and much has been gained in this enterprise. By looking at the academic "holy trinity" of race, social class, and gender as they are constructed on the screen, we see past the narratives of the screenplays to the ideological underpinnings that are the foundation of any movie's message(s). Furthermore, film scholars, fruitfully and to great effect, have been examining aspects of the film industry that previously

i

were largely ignored in our field: the means and politics of film production and distribution, audience reception, the role and influence of popular film criticism, film's intersections with other media, and many other modes of approach stemming from particularities of historical, sociological, and cultural situation.

This collection of essays on American film seeks to extend that academic dialogue. Although many of the chapters in this volume focus on one film, these pieces go far beyond close readings as they approach the films as matrices of intersecting voices located in particular socio-cultural moments and participating in significant historical trajectories. All of these essays insightfully examine how specific films have functioned in American history, their provenance, and their subsequent effects (potential or actual). Although a wide range of films is covered in this collection, from *A Raisin in the Sun* to *Thelma and Louise*, the films were all, within their genres, popular successes, and several of the films, like *Blade Runner*, have become iconic. It is not surprising, then, that every study in the volume exemplifies Stuart Hall's assertion that there is a double-stake in popular culture": the perpetual threat of the "double movement of containment and resistance" within the artifacts it produces. Hall, a socialist cultural theorist, argues that

> there is a continuous and necessarily uneven and unequal struggle, by dominant culture, constantly to disorganise and reorganise popular culture; to enclose and confine its definitions and forms within a more inclusive range of dominant forms. There are points of resistance; there are also moments of supersession. This is the dialectic of cultural struggle. In our time, it goes on continuously, in the complex lines of resistance and acceptance, refusal and capitulation, which make the field of culture a sort of constant battlefield.[1] (233)

As the authors in this collection argue, many films are engaged in this battle both internally (within their own narratives) and externally (with the dominant cultural ideologies). For instance, *Thelma and Louise* overtly contests patriarchal norms in late twentieth-century American society; however, as David Russell asserts, the film simultaneously, and in perhaps less obvious ways, reinforces some of the hegemonic ideas it is attempting to refute. Thus, there is both "resistance and acceptance." Similarly, Anil

Narine suggests that *Blade Runner* reveals cultural anxieties about social class unrest and immigration during a time of economic crisis in a way that supports popular racist and classist stereotypes, but it also posits a fundamental connection between beings that, if embraced, could engender radical egalitarianism.

Sometimes, the essay itself, rather than the film, is the "weapon" in the battle Hall describes. Vernon Shetley, for example, argues here that the much-lauded box office smash *Saving Private Ryan* powerfully communicates a retrograde, monolithic, and potentially dangerous ideal of masculinity that many viewers might absorb without notice. Shetley engages in the cultural struggle by unveiling the persistence of pernicious stereotypes in an extremely popular film. Cinema scholar Steven Ross, in his introduction to the volume *Movies and American Society*, notes that in the past few decades, "European and American scholars [have shown] how movies and other forms of mass culture [serve] as contested terrains of resistance and accommodation to the dominant and alternative ideas and values of society" (7). This is precisely the dialogue in which the authors participate in this collection. Perhaps, a movie enthusiast might say, this kind of detailed analysis and revelation of the challenging and disturbing aspects of the films we watch could dampen, or even ruin, "the joy of looking," to use a Mulvey-inspired phrase. However, if we refuse to examine the ideological implications of the films we watch, we are doomed – as individuals, as communities, and as a nation – to persist in our ignorant stereotypes and prejudices, in our oppression of "others," in our narcissistic self-justification of the damage we do in our spheres of influence, from the familial to the global.

The ineluctable, intricate, and intimate connections between film, politics, and history are made evident by a 1943 report, filed by an FBI special agent, that assesses the potential threat of film being used as political propaganda; its claims, though grandiose, may hold true to this day: "[T]he motion picture industry is beginning to be recognized as one of the greatest, if not the very greatest, influence upon the minds and culture, not only of the people of the United States, but of the entire world" ("Communist Political Influence and Activities in the Motion Picture Business in Hollywood, California," qtd. in Ross 214). This report, both its text and its very existence, underscores the importance of film in the history of the United States, and, inversely, the significance of the histories of America and its citizens as they are depicted on film.

The essays in this volume deal with the intersection of American history and the movies it has spawned. The articles grapple with the complex web of ideas and ideologies surrounding the issues of race, class, gender, ethnicity, and religion that arise in the films being examined. As I have stated, the films discussed in this book are predominantly "popular," released to the mass audience in the United States, and thus have a great deal of cultural relevance and resonance. With the partial exception of Brian Ireland's chapter on Hawaii films, which covers a lengthy span of time to trace the historical development of a genre, the films that appear in this volume are part of post-World War II American culture, a contradictory period replete with oppressive containment as well as intense questioning. As our authors show, even in the postmodern era of supposedly infinite readings and possibilities, popular film has a tendency to reify certain destructive ideologies, even while challenging other hegemonic structures.

Chapter One, "X Marks the Spot: The Crucible of Economics, Conspiracy, and Gender in *The X Files*," by Valerie Holliday, is an excellent example of this phenomenon of "refusal and capitulation" within the same text. However, unlike the other essays here, Holliday examines a television series, the popular, long-running *X Files*. The show seems to subvert dominant gender paradigms by reversing the assignment of "masculine" and "feminine" roles: the male Mulder is led by intuition and believes in the supernatural while the female Scully is the hard scientist, a trained physician, who has been called upon to monitor and debunk Mulder's detective work. As these two FBI agents try to solve the mysteries of the X-Files, their very different narratives seem to be equal, neither taking precedent over the other; therefore, truth is always deferred, in true postmodern fashion. This deferral also translates into the sexual tension between the partners that continues for many seasons, preventing a resolution to Mulder's "Oedipal conflict" and challenging the symbolic order of the nuclear family. Holliday argues that the series' demise begins when the creators make *The X Files* film in 1998 and succumb to the pressures inherent in the film medium to resolve the tensions and questions, forcing Mulder and Scully into the dominant symbolic order from which the series had so carefully removed them. Using psychoanalytic and postmodern theories, Holliday interrogates the ways in which *The X Files* television series capitulated to capitalist market imperatives in conjunction with its cinematic metamorphosis.

In our second chapter, Brian Ireland discusses the long and fascinating history of Hawaii in American film in an essay entitled, "'Enchanted Island': Hawaii, and Other American Fantasies." Ireland cites a plethora of movies, from the silents through Michael Bay's blockbuster *Pearl Harbor* in 2001, to illustrate his arguments regarding the agenda of films set in Hawaii. He divides these films into three periods – pre-World War II, post-World War II, and the late 1950s-1960s – and astutely ties each period and its films to the major events that shape these eras, such as the attack on Pearl Harbor and the historical Supreme Court decision in the *Brown v. The Board of Education of Topeka* case in 1954. These and several other momentous events in American history resulted in major shifts in the way the film industry used Hawaii to communicate its own agendas. In Ireland's words, "Cinematic depictions of Hawaii in war and peace, are less concerned with accuracy than they are with portraying Hawaii according to the needs of those on the U.S. mainland." Whether that translates into depictions of "savage" native Hawaiians in a paradisical landscape or to Hawaii shown as a haven of racial harmony, Hawaii on film has always been a fantasy. Through a sweeping account of Hawaii's cinematic history as well as closer examination of films such as *Hawaii Calls* (1938), *Big Jim McLain* (1952*), From Here To Eternity* (1953), and *Midway* (1976), Ireland illuminates Hawaii's status as ever-changing signifier.

In "John Wayne and the Queer Frontier: Deconstructions of the Classic Cowboy Narrative during the Vietnam War," our third chapter, Christopher Le Coney and Zoe Trodd argue that the metanarrative of the American frontier myth, including the crucial icon of the cowboy, was used to legitimate Vietnam, but by 1969, countercultural cowboy narratives were being filmed that questioned the "heteronormative" nature of the whole Western genre. Le Coney and Trodd use John Wayne and several of his films as touchstones for the cowboy and Western generic form respectively. However, by 1968, they assert, the war in Vietnam "had begun to undermine Americans' confidence in their classic cowboy and Indian narratives; cultural myths of an Anglo-American aggressor who always triumphed over the colored Other." Consequently, many in the civil rights and feminist movements connected their oppression inside the borders of their nation with the war overseas. It was in this cultural climate that the films *Midnight Cowboy* and *Lonesome Cowboys*, both released in 1969, were made. Le Coney and Trodd investigate these films in light of their reception history and the countercultures of the moment as well as analyzing the varying impact each of these films has had on the following generations of Westerns and the myths they represent.

Karl Martin's essay, "The Plagues of Egypt in the Promised Land: Paul Thomas Anderson's *Magnolia*," uses the structuralist idea of definition through binary opposition to examine the ways in which the film *Magnolia* comments on the New Israel (New World)/Egypt (or Babylon) dichotomy. Martin's study, like Le Coney and Trodd's, refers to a metanarrative of American history: the idea that America is the Promised Land. The intersecting narratives of *Magnolia*, like those in our own lives, refuse to validate that metanarrative; Americans, therefore, deny or attempt to ignore the pain of their own suffering in order to appear as if they have achieved the American dream in the land of infinite promise. In this way, Martin argues, the film addresses issues of national identity. Director P.T. Anderson presents several narratives depicting suffering people who have no voices to communicate their desperation and sorrow. *Magnolia* inverts the New Israel/Egypt binary, making the citizens of modern day Los Angeles victims of a biblical plague wrought upon Egypt, namely the raining of the frogs. This seemingly absurd event, which turns the American landscape into the oppressive Egypt, symbolically encourages the audience to "surrender the metaphor of America as a New World" and, as Aimee Mann's soundtrack insists, to "wise up." Through an examination of the complex narratives and prolific series of allusions in *Magnolia*, Martin contends that this film creates a space in which the destructive metanarratives of bourgeois nationalism can be transcended and, therefore, the truth about suffering can be expressed, opening a door to the possibility of hope and redemption.

Chapter five deals with the plight of Walter Lee Younger, Lorraine Hansberry's African American protagonist in her renowned play *A Raisin in the Sun* (1959). In 1961, the play was made into a film starring Sidney Poitier which differs little from its stage version and maintains the central focus on racism and the socio-economic dominance of the white male in Cold War culture. Michael P. Moreno, in his essay "Reifying Cold War (Sub)urban Systems: The Spatial Anatomy of Black Masculinity in *A Raisin in the Sun*," discusses the way in which the development of the suburbs after World War II caused a fragmenting of masculine identity for both white and black men. Moreno argues that *Raisin* "succinctly illustrates how black masculinity challenges and is challenged by white male hegemony, and how the fractured identity of the black male is rooted within a Cold War heterotopia of colliding masculine roles." Walter Lee attempts to establish himself as the responsible head of the family in both the urban and suburban environments, but struggles in both arenas. Morena asserts that the film problematically reinforces the image of suburbia as utopic space, the myth of the idyllic non-urban landscape, even as the narrative portrays Walter Lee's ultimate overcoming of the racism that threatens to keep him out of this idealized space. Therefore, *A Raisin in the Sun* simultaneously and paradoxically resists and condemns racism while accepting the myth that prosperity can only be realized in a space reserved for whites, abandoning urban spaces to decay and desolation.

Notes

1. It is important to acknowledge that Hall's definition of *popular culture* differs from what most contemporary scholars mean when they use this term; his bifurcation of "dominant culture" and "popular culture" is problematic in that the boundaries between these two are not only permeable but often invisible or absent altogether. Nevertheless, his argument that popular culture is a "battlefield" in which resistance and acceptance are in constant conflict is both useful and insightful.

Works Cited

Hall, Stuart. "Notes on Deconstructing 'the Popular'." *People's History and Socialist Theory.* Ed. Raphael Samuel. London: Routledge, 1981. 227-40.
Ross, Steven J., ed. *Movies and Mass Society.* Oxford, UK: Blackwell, 2002.

1

X Marks the Spot:
The Crucible of Economics, Conspiracy, and Gender in *The X Files*

Valerie Holliday

In every sense, the study of gender, evolving as it has from feminism, has been a historical materialist undertaking. The phenomenological quality of feminism – its starting point always in lived experience – has at all times been profoundly evident. No matter what question a feminist analytic attempts to answer, it always returns to the question, "What is the condition of women?" It is not, however, a structural necessity of feminism to consider the economic imperatives of late capitalism. Certainly, a number of feminists do practice historical materialist feminism; that this is so does not imply a necessity. I argue that it is absolutely essential for any theorist, as a matter of responsibility, to work assiduously to make a historical materialist feminist dialectic an inevitability. Marxists tend in the main to treat feminism and gender studies as a nicety but not a necessity in their studies of late capitalism; feminists tend to bristle at the idea that women's and gender studies ought to be integrated with other theoretical paradigms. But this conventional separatist attitude is enormously counterproductive in any political agenda. And yet historical materialist feminism is still not enough. Psychoanalysis has taught us much about the ways in which humans develop, and the ways in which we organize socially. Any meaningful political dialogue will account for these insights. Terry Eagleton has shown in *After Theory* that cultural theory is in danger of trivializing itself out of practical existence. His point here is precisely why I argue that we must take a rigorously dialectic approach to theory. And while he indicates that poststructuralism is passé, I would argue that gender studies is the way in which we will revitalize the absolutely essential and not at all passé theories of Marxism and psychoanalysis. By looking at *The X Files*, we can see the ways in which, in the light of feminism, gender works to foreclose on meaningful and productive political discussion. The point precisely is that this foreclosure is *after* second- and third-wave feminism. How insidious is gender oppression, then, when we cannot put our finger now on outmoded or oppressive representations? This essay seeks to explore how gender oppression has evolved to accommodate revolutions in media representations of women and precisely how this accommodation has been made tenable by economic forces.

At first glance, *The X Files* appears to be subversive: its fundamental storyline articulates elaborately the inner workings of government conspiracy in the United States. And in many ways the series is subversive, but less for its exploration of government conspiracy and much more for its remarkable tenacity in holding conventional gender ideology at bay for so many years, a point to which I will turn in detail shortly. Herbert Marcuse's notion of repressive tolerance best expresses both the phenomenon of the *X Files* franchise in the American market and the diegetic condition of the two main characters, Fox Mulder and Dana Scully. The X files themselves are the unsolved cases that the FBI will not close – they *can* close them if they wish; they choose not to. Powerful officials have kept the X files open in order to keep Fox Mulder both busy *and* inside the FBI, where he may be safely controlled. For Marcuse, tolerance that augments repression is not tolerance at all – it is, in fact, typical in democratic societies for "the people [to] tolerate the government, which in turn tolerates opposition within the framework determined by the constituted authorities" (83). The FBI tolerates Fox Mulder, not as a condition of Mulder's freedom but rather precisely the opposite – to limit what he can and will do but specifically *under the pretense* of permitting his free acquisition of knowledge. Mulder is, of course, aware of his positioning in the agency; he knows he is situated inside of a particular cultural, political, and bureaucratic structure with no possibility of acting outside of it *and* fully accepts this positioning even as it reifies his own fictionality.[1] Mulder is acutely aware of the way in which he is ideologically constructed and is (mainly) content to work within that construction. Mulder, thus, spends the entirety of the series working to use the repressive tolerance employed to prevent his subversive acts as precisely the means by which he will subvert the system.

While Mulder is emblematic of the institutional use of repressive tolerance, the appearance of the series is itself a case of repressive tolerance. That is, the series represents the American government generally and the FBI specifically in a very negative way; this representation is in every sense *permitted* by the hegemonic structure. Media representations are controlled and suppressed routinely for a variety of reasons, most often for national security and interests, but not always. The cancellation of the CBS broadcast of the television film *The Reagans* is just one case in point. Thus, in a stunning series of multiple mirror images, *The X Files* is a case of repressive tolerance in action, in which it actually *represents* the systematic use of repressive tolerance by the American government *precisely* in order to perpetuate a policy of repressive tolerance with regard to theories of government conspiracy.

This perpetual contradiction between repression and permission is the hallmark of capitalism: rather than couching the phenomenon in Marcuse's term "repressive tolerance," it is more appropriate in this context to call it *necessary subversion*. This conundrum is characteristic of capitalism. Ellen Wood in her 2003 study of global capital, *Empire of Capital*, notes that it is the peculiar circumstance of the United States that it must both maintain the singularly and overwhelmingly dominant military force in the world in order to preserve the stability and order necessary for global capital to thrive and at the same time is obligated, in the interest of preserving markets, not to use that power or at least not use it excessively. The 2001 war in Afghanistan was not so much a step in the "war on terror" but rather a show of force for non-compliant countries like North Korea. The necessity of preserving global markets is precisely analogous to the phenomenon of necessary subversion. It is less that the hegemonic power is intelligently and deceptively tolerating subversion as an intentionally repressive gesture and more that it is limited as to what it can do to repress subversion while still preserving its dominance. Subversion is, in this sense, an unpleasant event that must, by the virtue of capitalist imperatives, be tolerated. Of course, the hegemonic power may at any time decide to use direct force to quell subversion; to dwell on this fact is, however, to miss the hope involved in a theory of necessary subversion. Ellen Wood notes, "Capitalism is uniquely driven by economic imperatives: on the one hand, the propertylessness of producers, which compels them to sell their labour power for a wage, and, on the other, the subjection of appropriators to the compulsions of the market, which oblige them to compete and accumulate" (89). However much the hegemony might want it otherwise, capitalist imperatives drive the need for tolerance because the market demands it. Permission to subvert is granted, not by virtue of "democratic" imperatives, but only by virtue of the imperative of capital accumulation.

Indeed, these imperatives may be seen in the occasion of *The X Files* itself. The series ran for nine seasons, during which time it grounded Fox Network as a viable competitor in the broadcast market. David Duchovny, who played Fox Mulder, said once that *The X Files* is not *on* Fox Network – it *is* the network. By around seasons six and seven, that remark was arguably true. The series spoke directly to the culture of conspiracy that has characterized the American post-World War II period and as such it was an enormous market success. Its tendency to challenge the legitimacy of the American government and its bureaucracies was hardly a high price to pay in the face of the huge market shares that it promised and indeed returned. Ironically, but not at all surprising, Fox's news bureau is notoriously the most reactionary and conservative of the major news sources. No doubt the success of the "subversive" *X Files* series contributed to the capital base that made Fox News Network possible.

The X Files embodies the dialectical tension of capitalism in a myriad of ways. The series premiered three years after the Soviet Union collapsed. Before the end of the Cold War, the economic condition of the globe was characterized by the standoff between two major powers. After the Cold War, the United States asserted fully its global supremacy; this global condition changed significantly the discourse of conspiracy in the United States. Without the oppositional structure of Cold War politics, the substance of conspiracy narrative shifted to represent the centerlessness of the American power structure. Often, Mulder and Scully fail to draw any narratively satisfying answers, even though they are able with a reasonable degree of certainty to assure themselves that somewhere in the deep recesses of American government is a vast countersubversive movement. Even in the less conspiratorial and more paranormal plot arcs they are often unable to provide an empirical explanation for the phenomena they find.

More importantly, however, *The X Files* marks an important shift in conspiracy culture from the dialectic of Cold War politics to the dialectic of *gender*. Indeed, the series in many ways articulates the theoretical problematic of Marxism and gender ideology with which this essay is finally concerned. On the one hand, the series works successfully and at the same time fails to demonstrate a politics of necessary subversion. On the other hand, the show constructs a narrative that is for the entire nine seasons driven by the romantic tension between Mulder and Scully – even though the possibility of their becoming romantically involved is not seriously presented until around the sixth and seventh seasons, at the time of the film release. But even more than romantic tension is the gender construction of each character: Mulder is the intuitive conspiracy theorist. Mulder majored in psychology at Oxford, a profession not exclusively the province of women but by no means totally dominated by men. Scully is the scientist; she is a trained medical doctor and takes the primacy of empirical evidence very seriously. She is assigned by the powers that be in the pilot episode as Mulder's partner, for the express purpose of "debunking" his theories as so much conspiracy hype. For all practical purposes, Scully is intended to be the husband to the madwoman. Right from the beginning, the series shifts the tension of necessary subversion onto the tension of gender politics. The true crisis is one of masculinity: Mulder embodies this crisis. For the majority of the nine years, the dialectic of gender both sustains and deflects the implications of the show's subversiveness. It does so in part by reversing the conventional gender roles of the two main characters. But simple role reversal does not guarantee a feminist text. We need the categories of psychoanalysis to unpack the oppression that arises out of shifting economic imperatives.

There is a close relationship, for Freud, between paranoia and hysteria. The symptoms of both of these illnesses are caused mainly by a repressed homosexual wish, so both paranoia and hysteria reveal bisexuality, a point that Freud felt he could not stress enough. The function of repression works differently in each illness. Whereas the paranoid's fantasies tend to irrupt into consciousness, the hysterical fantasies tend not to return so quickly, if at all. More technically, hysteria is characterized by its tendency toward *condensation*. In *Dora: An Analysis of a Case of Hysteria*, Freud finds condensation in Dora when, very often, her dream imagery served to represent several different and intersecting repressed wishes – what Freud called overdetermination. He isolated "switching words," which served as something like railroad track switches, in her speech and her dreams on which these intersecting fantasies pivoted (82).[2] By contrast, paranoia tends toward *decomposition* – or the fragmenting of repressed wishes. But Freud is extremely quick to point out that the process of decomposition in the paranoiac is more complicated because the paranoiac decomposes *after* he has gone through some unconscious

6

process of condensation. He says, "Paranoia decomposes just as hysteria condenses. Or *rather*, paranoia resolves once more into their elements the products of the condensations and identifications which are effected in the unconscious" (*CW12* 49, italics mine). The idea of the conspiracy theorist as paranoid fails to register the hysteric component of condensation. After all, the conspiracy theorist is such precisely because he seeks and finds intersections. Hysterical condensation in the conspiracy theorist shows itself inexorably in the form of a reasserted Oedipal drama and resolution. In order for the conspiracy theorist to cure himself of paranoia, he must condense his intersecting fantasies into a coherent story. The ordering narrative for the conspiracy theorist is the narrative of Lacan's rereading of the Oedipal complex: the symbolic order as the Law of the Father. The symbolic order is reinstituted in the conspiracy theorist's move from paranoia to hysteria.

In *The X Files*, there is a paranoid-hysterical male and a professional female who interact such that romantic tension is always implicit but never realized (until after the film). The structural components of the symbolic order and its destabilization in Mulder and Scully's psychodrama are evident from the pilot episode (air date 10 September 1993). The pilot is especially significant in the development of Mulder and Scully's relationship, because it is there that the conditions of their work relationship are established; these conditions will remain for essentially the entire series, even in later seasons when Scully finally gives up her role as "debunker" of Mulder's work. The pilot opens with scenes from the Oregon case that Scully and Mulder will investigate: recently graduated high school students are mysteriously dying in the Oregon forest, with evidence of paranormal activity being the cause. Scully appears first in the pilot: she converses with two unnamed administrative figures in the FBI chain of command. During this meeting, Scully is given her assignment to work on the X Files, which is to "assist" Mulder and observe the "validity" of the work. To this charge, Scully replies, "Am I to understand that you want me to debunk the X Files project, sir?" The senior FBI official answers, "Agent Scully, we trust you'll make the proper scientific analysis." With this exchange, the series sets up the structure of its dual political premises: first, that science is to be dubiously set against other, less "valid" kinds of knowledge, and second, that a woman will escort this more "valid" knowledge into the plot line. These two premises are structurally dependent on one another; as such, it is important to understand the implications of the former premise in order to understand how the latter premise obtains. Scully presents the more "valid" or empirical, and thus male, knowledge. Mulder embodies feminine, intuitive knowledge.

It is not that the senior FBI officials do not believe Mulder's claims; it is rather that they *exactly* believe them, because they know Mulder is right. The Pentagon and the FBI have called Scully forward to debunk Mulder's work and produce "reports" that present scientific explanations for his theories, in order to obfuscate the truth. Scully's assignment, to the FBI, is not to find objective truth; it is to find a narrative that *looks like* objective truth. *The X Files* is in this regard a fully postmodern cultural artifact. In *The Postmodern Condition*, Francois Lyotard points out that all knowledge comes in the form of narrative, that is, in the form of language; he thus remakes epistemology into a study of linguistics. This narrative view of truth seems to suggest that only localized "truths" may be found – there is no "truth out there," as the series' slogan says. However, Fredric Jameson points out in the foreword to the 1984 edition of *The Postmodern Condition* that "this seeming contradiction [between local narratives and the generalized function of narrative] can be resolved, I believe, by taking a further step that Lyotard seems unwilling to do in the present text, namely to posit, not the disappearance of the great master-narratives, but their passage underground as it were, their continuing but now *unconscious* effectivity as a way of 'thinking about' and acting in our current situation" (xii, original italics). There is indeed a master narrative in *The X Files*, and both Mulder and Scully pursue it regularly. That each of them represents an instance of a particular localized narrative does nothing to undermine the existence of the extraterrestrial conspiracy of which they find much evidence. The impossibility of either Scully's or Mulder's narrative to trump the other makes *The X Files* an exemplary case of Lyotard's postmodern knowledge; the positing of conspiracy in *The X Files*, and the nature of that positing, is fundamentally the work of Jameson's submerged political narratives. This master narrative, that the truth is "out there," directs all of Scully and Mulder's activities.

The sense that the series makes of the condition of knowledge in the postmodern period depends on the radical problematization of the symbolic order. The series destabilizes traditional knowledge in a Lyotardian sense, but only to the degree that the series, at least in the early seasons, defers the resolution of Mulder's Oedipal conflict. In this way, a critique of *The X Files*, or of any cultural artifact, is useful only to the degree that it moves dialectically from theoretical paradigm to theoretical paradigm. So far, I have shown that with adjustments Marcuse's notion of repressive tolerance is useful in understanding *The X Files* both diegetically and materially; Lyotard's and Jameson's model of human knowledge helps explain the epistemological implications of Marcuse's politics; we then turn to Lacanian and Freudian psychoanalysis to explain how gender functions as the fulcrum upon which human knowledge pivots. None of these theoretical paradigms in this context is useful without the others. I have no doubt that a dialectical critique of gender is not the last word in any theoretical paradigm; surely some other theoretical paradigm is required to further this political cultural critique, and this essay suggests that a critical apparatus must be developed to avoid the degradation of critical theory into irrelevance, as Terry Eagleton has argued in *After Theory*. It is my contention that Marxist theorists such as Jameson have all too often elided the material reality of gender, and often a critique of capital fails to register the ways in which gender is integral to every phase of capitalist accumulation. That is, the capitalist subject, such as he often appears in Marxist critique, is rarely categorized by gender. In fact, however, the capitalist subject *is* gendered, and that gender categorization has an effect on the way in which the capitalist subject moves around in capitalist society. The gender of the capitalist subject is inexorably a feature of the capitalist subject's identity.

Mulder represents the *masculine* capitalist subject in crisis, and this crisis in addition to being an economic crisis is also a psychosexual one. He is wary, sardonic, and suspicious of everyone – in fact, he is often told by his counter-counterinsurgent sources to "trust no one." While the series does not represent in any direct way the effects or symptoms of globalized capital, Mulder nonetheless represents the anxiety caused by the decomposition of the polarized global economy of the Cold War. Mulder is an absolutely critical element of the series' success. Indeed, actor David Duchovny is so closely identified with the character of Mulder that when his contract negotiations failed late in the series run, his replacement, actor Robert Patrick, could not sustain either the story as it was originally constructed or the fan base. Mulder's replacement, Agent Doggett, was not sufficiently hysterical to work as a meaningful mirror image for the masculine capitalist subject; he failed to quilt together the evidence of conspiracy the way in which Mulder did, leaving much of that work to the by then eminently convinced Scully. Mulder/Duchovny were love objects into which the paranoid conspiracy theorist viewer, that the series constructs, invested his libido. Doggett/Patrick, by contrast, were rejected. But by himself, Mulder cannot sustain the diegesis; the series plot line must provide some sort of stabilizing resolution to the interrelated crises of knowledge, globalized economy, and human subjectivity. It is to this purpose that the character of Scully is exclusively directed.

Scully embodies all that is good about empirical doubt. She questions Mulder's every conclusion in the pilot episode (and for many seasons after that); what is more interesting is the degree to which, and the manner in which, she *considers* his conclusions. The Oregon high school graduates who have either died or receded into various states of living decay all show one common feature as the result of whatever events they have suffered – they all have two distinguishable marks on their lower right hips, marks that look much like a snake bite, but more pronounced. Scully doubts Mulder's conclusion that these marks are evidence of extraterrestrial abduction, and she gives him ample possibilities as alternatives. One evening in her hotel room, Scully discovers two or three of these marks on her lower right hip; she runs noticeably shaken to Mulder's hotel room to have him look at them. She slips off her robe to reveal to Mulder that she is in only her panties and bra (unnecessarily enough); Mulder is momentarily distracted by her nearly nude body, but when she looks back at him to see what he is doing, he shakes his interest in her body and squats down to examine the marks closely. After a moment he declares that they are nothing more than mosquito bites. In spite of this good news, Scully is still visibly shaken and falls into Mulder's arms in relief. He is stunned; they have only met just days ago, and this case is their first together. Scully's ingenuous show of intimacy is all but entirely out of place. And yet Mulder is receptive; when she says she must sit down for a moment, he says, "sure," and sits down humbly and quietly with her at the table in order to help calm her down.

Scully's positioning should not, however, be understood as an infantilization, at least not in the seasons prior to the release of *The X Files* film. Scully is a trained medical doctor; as such, she is more educated than Mulder. When she speaks medically, Mulder listens and respects her opinion – he, in fact, takes it to be the unproblematic truth. More importantly, however, Scully takes care of Mulder at least as much as Mulder protects her. For instance, in the second episode, entitled "Deep Throat," Mulder and Scully discover unusual testing activities at a military air base in Idaho; in order to discover more, Mulder trespasses onto the base. Eventually, he sees an aircraft that is able to change direction quickly, hover indefinitely, and travel silently. This aircraft is a military experiment derived from, according to Mulder, the wreckage of a UFO more than forty years earlier. After Mulder sees the aircraft, he is apprehended by military personnel, restrained, drugged, and subjected to a memory eradication procedure. Scully, for her part, works assiduously to save Mulder from the grasp of the military; she takes a military official hostage at gunpoint and orders him to take her to Mulder. He does, and the military uneventfully releases Mulder into Scully's custody at the base gate. He is disoriented, confused, and almost childlike. It is only Scully who can pull him out of the military's grasp and protect him maternally in his bewildered state.

This scene marks the collision of two powerful branches of government as well as the destabilization of the symbolic order. Scully and Mulder bear the authority of the Federal Bureau of Investigation. Nonetheless, the military summarily trumps this power by roughing Mulder and Scully up (in an earlier scene) and then abducting Mulder and performing medical procedures on him to which he obviously does not consent. The military destroys the evidence they have obtained, and they return to Washington bereft of any proof of the military's dangerous experiments. Their superiors frown upon their conclusions. When the military and the FBI clash, the symbolic order is devastated; there is no law to which Scully and Mulder may appeal, no higher authority to which they may turn to sort out this conflict. Their own authority as agents of the FBI is simply irrelevant. The State in this case fails to represent order in the global capitalized structure of the production of war material. In the movement of the phallus between the regulatory FBI and the productive military, Mulder cathects to the mother in order to quell the anxiety.

But if Mulder is by turns the father and Scully the mother, this is not to suggest that the series concretizes them into these categories. The fluidity of the two characters allows the series to examine the United States governmental infrastructure with a view to psychoanalytic and capitalist categories, at least for about seven seasons. The series does lapse into a finalizing enactment of the symbolic order in the final three seasons when Scully and Mulder struggle to and eventually form a sort of nuclear family. This shift in the series' focus coincides with the production of the film, *The X Files: Fight the Future*. Chris Carter admits freely that the film production occurred during the regular production schedule of the television series and as such was incredibly intense and stressful. Just as importantly, the *X Files'* production team shifted the mode of production from television to film and then back again. The technical parameters of film mandate a different set of plot paradigms – most obviously, much has to be resolved in two hours. Moreover, film demands more spectacle. The creators could not rely on the patient tenacity of regular weekly viewers to drive the film's success. Indeed, much of the television series' success was the result of its ability to both resolve and confound at the same time, over a protracted period of time. The film was not allowed this luxury. No doubt someone saw the potential profit in a film version of *The X Files*, and so the beginning of the series' demise was put into play. There was no way that the series could return comfortably to its original premise after the film. While the creators worked hard to make the film a stand alone phenomenon, it was not possible to do so in a milieu where long-term plotline was so eminently important. In this way, it is easy to see how market imperatives effectively warped the plot development of an otherwise successful television franchise. It is the nature of capitalism to destroy that which engenders its success; the capitalist dialectic was fully at work in the production history of *The X Files*. The point for the present discussion is especially that the capitalist dialectic of production forced the hand of the creators to enact in the series a final entry into the symbolic order for Mulder and Scully, and the resolution of Mulder's Oedipal conflict.

The pre-release hype around the movie focused a good bit of attention on the matter of whether Scully and Mulder would finally kiss. For the fan base at least, it seemed that the omnipresent tension between Mulder and Scully's deeply committed, professional, non-sexual friendship and their latent sexual desire was of eminent importance. The urge to resolve this tension was not necessarily universal, but the concern with it was nonetheless captivating. That tension, after all, sustained and nurtured the success of the series for the first six seasons. One of the trailers for the film gives a clip from the scene in which Scully and Mulder *almost* kiss to rouse this curiosity. Regular viewers would appreciate the tease if non-viewers did not entirely grasp the significance of the clip. Before the film was released on 19 June 1998, the question of the desublimation of Scully and Mulder's sexual attraction, or even whether it was present to be sublimated in the first place, was fully visible. Much pressure, therefore, was on the writers, Chris Carter and Frank Spotniz, to satisfy this viewer desire. There was no time like the film production to play dangerously with the nature of Scully and Mulder's relationship. A close-up, two-head shot of an impending kiss was absolutely required in the previews. The trouble was that series creator Carter knew that sexual involvement between Mulder and Scully was counterproductive to the television series' success. In interviews, he has stated that he never intended for the two main characters to become romantically involved as it would have interfered with the show's ability to elaborate on conspiracy theories. He was thus caught between two substantially different modes of plot production with two entirely different sets of market imperatives: on the one hand, the television series had to maintain its successful market franchise by sustaining a significant viewer base over time. On the other hand, the film had to bring both regular viewers and non-viewers into the theater for a very short period of time. In this shift in the mode of production of *The X Files* for the sake of market (not to mention media) imperatives was a reassertion of the symbolic order based on gender categories. Subsequent to the film, the series attempted to undo or unassert the symbolic order for the sake of the series' success but ultimately failed.

The film also promised to explain more clearly the exact nature of the conspiracy that Carter had been developing for six seasons and in that regard was fairly successful. In essence, an alien race has been residing on earth in a dormant state for millions of years, while waiting, presumably, for a suitable host to emerge so that they might dwell comfortably and ultimately dominate the terran landscape. In the late 1940s and early 1950s, government officials, not necessarily exclusively American, were contacted by these aliens and forced to employ a kind of diplomacy under pressure; they formed a secret group to cooperate with the aliens. But in 1998, at the time of the film, the aliens began to use humans to gestate, rather than simply as hosts for hybridization. The film begins when the secret group discovers that an alien has gestated in four human beings in a small community in North Texas. Mulder and Scully first appear in the film during a bomb threat investigation in Dallas, Texas. Mulder discovers the bomb in the building across the street from the federal building, where the bomb threat was actually called in. Mulder finds himself locked in the canteen with the bomb that is set in the vending machine. He has fifteen minutes to get out, and shortly Scully rescues him; that each of them takes turns rescuing the other is consistent with the regular storyline of the television series. The ordinary gender structure of the series does not prioritize the dominance of the one over the other. What Scully and Mulder only realize later is that the bombing in Dallas is directly related to the conspiracy involving the aliens. That is, the bodies of the four human beings who had been used for alien gestation in North Texas were in a

FEMA office in that building. As Mulder and Scully slowly come to discover that the bombing was a cover-up for the alien conspiracy, Mulder has a chance later to say things like, "This all goes back to Dallas," which is the line that JFK assassination conspiracy theorists give to explain the connections that they see.

The division of labor in the film largely remains the same as in the television series. Mulder, because he is seen by FBI and government administration as irresponsible, is left out of the committee hearings established to investigate the bombing in Dallas. Scully is the voice for the pair in these hearings. Likewise, Scully continues to be the voice of rational, scientific, empiricist inquiry and Mulder consistently defers to her opinion on forensic matters. Mulder, for his part, continues to be the voice of intuition, pursuing esoteric leads, discovering unempirical truths, and meeting with obscure sources in dark alleys. There is, however, a barely perceptible but nonetheless very clear shift in the balance of mutual care in the film. That is, while about nine minutes of film time is spent on Scully's rescue of Mulder from the bomb site, fully the last thirty minutes of the film is spent on Mulder's rescue of Scully from the alien/government project site in Antarctica. In the television series, these rescue efforts are ordinarily fairly balanced; but in the film, they are disproportionate, and not only is Mulder's rescue of Scully bigger and more profound, it serves to close the film, which gives it a privileged position in the trajectory of the plot. Indeed, the last scene of the film indicates that this struggle between secret government operations and the FBI is ultimately Mulder's alone.

The Smoking Man brings a message to Conrad Strughold (Armin Mueller-Stahl), one of the key figures in the government collusion with the aliens, indicating that the X Files are being reopened by the committee investigating the Dallas bombing. During that conversation, the Smoking Man tells Strughold that Mulder is determined now, to which Strughold replies, "He is but one man. One man alone cannot fight the future." There is a sense in which the X-Files have always been Mulder's and not Scully's, but in the context of Mulder's profound, film-sized rescue of Scully, this scene resonates profoundly with the message that Scully is in the service of Mulder as a narrative device. This condition marks the beginning of the end of the deferral of the symbolic order. In Mulder and Scully's final scene in the film, Scully recommits herself to Mulder's cause. After the committee orders her reassignment to Salt Lake City, Utah (presumably a damnation), before she is abducted by the government,

Scully announces to Mulder that she is quitting the FBI to practice medicine, that it is time for her to start living her life for herself. In this context, Scully's later decision to remain with the X Files looks more and more like service to Mulder and not to the administrators who had asked her years before to "debunk" Mulder's work. A substantive shift in Scully's motivation occurs in the film in this moment, one that will change the direction of the series seasons that follow. Before the film she was committed both to the protocol and directives of the FBI and at the same time to a sincere regard for Mulder's work; after the film she is committed to nothing other than Mulder qua conspiracy theorist, friend, and eventually pseudo-husband. If there was a tension between Scully's internal motivations initially, after the film those tensions are gone. Before the film, the symbolic order is consistently destabilized in turns by shifting institutional power structures and Mulder's persistently unresolved Oedipal conflict. In this way, we can clearly see the seamlessness between material market imperatives, modes of production, and gender construction. The shift in the mode of story construction forced the hand of the creators to accede to the reenactment of the entry into the symbolic order. To point out that *The X Files* is a fictional construction is to entirely miss the point that it is a market *product* and as such is the result of a mode of production.

Scully experiences a change of symbolic order and the film does everything to represent and empower that change. The pivotal scene that makes this change possible is not surprisingly the scene in which Mulder and Scully almost kiss. Scully visits Mulder at his apartment to tell him that she has been reassigned to Salt Lake City and that she is therefore quitting the FBI. Mulder protests doggedly; he follows her out into the hallway where they have an exchange befitting two people who care deeply for one another. He tells her that he needs her, and that he owes her everything and she owes him nothing. Scully's hand firmly clasps Mulder's neck, and Mulder takes Scully's face in his hands. Mulder leans in slowly to kiss her, but he is interrupted when Scully jumps suddenly from a sting on the back of the neck by an Africanized bee. The significance of this interruption is even more pronounced when one considers that this bee is part of the government-developed transit system for spreading the alien virus. Just the night before Scully and Mulder had been investigating a large, conspicuously misplaced corn crop in the middle of the Texas desert. At the center of that corn crop is a gigantic beekeeping facility (two domed tents that look like, as Mulder put it, "Jiffy

Pop poppers") where Scully picks up that Africanized bee. It stays under her collar for nearly twenty-four hours before stinging her at just the moment she and Mulder nearly succumb to sexual desire. Therefore, the thing that interrupts Scully and Mulder's sexual encounter is also the thing that will set the events leading up to the final rescue scene into motion. As I have argued, the final rescue scene is disproportionate and imbalanced and is the event that signals a change in Scully's place in the symbolic order. It follows, then, that the bee sting and subsequent alien infection are only appropriate as a sort of coitus interruptus. Instead of participating in a romantic encounter, Scully immediately goes into paralysis and Mulder eases her limp body onto the floor of the hallway. Scully must be utterly paralyzed in order for the film to make this subtle turn toward the assertion of Mulder as the law of the father.

Shifting Scully's motivation in the film was not enough to assert Mulder's dominance as the law of the father; David Duchovny, the actor who plays Mulder, began to heave his success around in the seventh season. The series was dependent on Duchovny as Mulder for its success; as such, Duchovny began to take advantage of this dependency by demanding more creative control. He wrote several scripts and directed some episodes. His dissatisfaction, however, continued to grow. He demanded that the shooting location be changed from Canada to Los Angeles so that he could be closer to his new wife, Tea Leoni – a move that proved to be devastating to the show's production, because production costs in Los Angeles are much higher than in Canada. Finally, his contract negotiations failed and by the end of the eighth season he was all but absent from the series.[3] He made guest appearances in the final season, but that was it. Duchovny's absence left the creators with a serious problem: Duchovny's Mulder attracted a huge fan base, and as such transferring this devotion to another character would prove to be difficult. Reactions to his replacement, Robert Patrick, were mixed. More importantly, though, for the present discussion, Mulder's absence made it difficult to carry Scully's motivation to its logical conclusion. Mulder's absence, and its concomitant disturbance to the symbolic order, was corrected by giving Scully a pregnancy in the eighth season, in the final episode of which she gives birth to her son William. The phallus moved for Scully from the law of the FBI, to the law of Mulder as father, to the assertion of baby as phallus.

All of Scully's prenatal and postnatal decisions refer exclusively to her concerns for her baby. Her interest in government malfeasance is governed only by this concern: if she has nothing to gain from involving herself in investigations, she does not do it. In the ninth season, when she becomes concerned that baby William is the result of a government project to create supersoldiers, she reluctantly becomes involved in Agent Doggett's investigation surrounding that project. Early in the ninth season, she is shown more in her apartment in domestic solitude with her child than she is anywhere else. She receives more guests there in the first three episodes of season nine than she does in the entire series run up to that point. Duchovny's absence from the series functions wholly as an absence of the phallus, which must be replaced in order to fulfill the primal scene that was set in motion in the film. The character of Mulder remained fully a part of the plot construction of the eighth and ninth seasons, even if Duchovny was not there to represent him. As such, the other characters refer often to the absent Mulder, wondering where he is, or attempting to get Scully to reveal where he is. He becomes finally a mystified enigma, creating a lack where otherwise none was before, a lack the baby William fills.

Speculation is plentiful on fan sites and series reviews about whether the series would have survived if Duchovny had not wrangled with the production. Certainly, key plot developments, namely Scully's new exclusive commitment to Mulder in the film, assisted in hastening the series to its conclusion before Duchovny ever began to complain. In season nine, Scully gives up her baby for adoption in order to protect him from danger. In this move, she gives up the phallus that she gained in season eight. This abandonment of the phallus is not, however, in itself a resolution. David Duchovny appears in the final episode of the series; in that episode, he and Scully become fugitives from both military and civilian justice. The series' final scene is of Mulder and Scully in a hotel room in New Mexico on the bed in a tender embrace. They have abandoned duty to the law in order to be together. The signifying phallus, the thing that gives order to human experience, is present – in the absence of Scully's baby, Mulder returns to take the position as phallus and as the organizing principle of both Scully's world and *The X Files* as a whole.

All through the nine-year run, *The X Files* was constructed such that it was to be understood as Mulder's story – the X Files were themselves Mulder's pet project, to which Scully was assigned in order to spy on Mulder. In truth, however, *The X Files* demonstrates an elaborate tale of gender, and an intricate replay of the primal scene. In this sense, because the feminine role is so vital to the dominance of the phallus, *The X Files* is in a demonstrative way the development of the story of gender. In many ways, it is Scully's story. In *The X Files*, the conspiracy theorist turns out to be unproblematically right; he also is understood by nearly everyone, except the important female figure, to be completely insane. He is perpetually caught in the epistemological abyss. It is the presence of a female that serves to ground his knowledge in a way that no other element of human experience can. It is only against the woman that the conspiracy theorist may assert the order of the phallus. Otherwise, he is caught in the damning real of his exemplary knowledge.

The X Files is indeed Scully's story – not in any overt way, however. In a cultural artifact that looks for all the world like a fully self-conscious postmodern examination, *The X Files* is unambiguously a demonstration of the fact that we are still in the historical moment of psychoanalysis. The psychoanalytic subject emerged roughly at the same time as the capitalist subject. That is, capital accumulation in Venice and the first use of manufactured mirrors both appeared in the sixteenth century. The emergence of a product which enabled humans to apprehend their own form more clearly than ever before marks the beginning of the Lacanian category of the mirror stage. We have not yet emerged from that period of human subjective development and experience. *The X Files* is to be commended for its rigorous exploration of the condition of human knowledge at the end of the twentieth century and at the beginning of the twenty-first. But Scully's positioning is fully instructive of the way in which the psychoanalytic category of gender remains underquestioned, in spite of the fact that the series appears to be self-conscious about the condition of women. Scully is a scientist, and as such is the sentinel of empirical certainty and rational doubt. This is a reversal of traditional gender roles if there ever was one. But simple reversals will not solve the problem of gender oppression. If the conspiracy theorist is emblematic of the postmodern age in his perpetual quest for and failure to find the truth, his unwavering distrust of the scripted and received story, his faith in unempirical knowledge, and even his neuroses about the globalized reach of late capitalism, our representations of him still necessitate the reenactment of the primal scene of the infant in conflict with the phallus.

Scully's function in *The X Files*, at the surface, is to play foil to Mulder's theories and provide a referent for tension. More importantly for any political and theoretical discussion, Scully's function is to mark the necessity of theory to turn its gaze repeatedly to the concerns that feminism originally brought to our attention. At its broadest, feminism asks us, "What is the condition of women?" We cannot return, however, to the second or even the third wave of feminism, or, even worse, assert that we are now "post-feminist." As theorists, we must find a way to move dialectically from theoretical paradigm to theoretical paradigm. In every case, we must ask of any work of art, any cultural artifact, any economic system, "What is the function of gender here?" In the case of *The X Files*, gender serves as a means by which the radical representation of the condition of human knowledge, in the form of the conspiracy theorist, may be summarily foreclosed. A materialist analysis of *The X Files* shows us that even in an economic sense, gender trumps the form when the forces of market imperatives act on a cultural phenomenon. When the mode of production of *The X Files* shifted from television to film, the resonant effect was for psychoanalytic categories of gender to dominate the plot direction. Without question, *The X Files* earmarks the way in which these three material *and* theoretical paradigms – historical materialism, psychoanalysis, and gender – intersect profoundly. Accordingly, any theoretical analysis of cultural artifacts such as *The X Files* must account for at least these human social and political categories.

We have succeeded in revolutionizing representations of women, Scully being one of only a number of representations of intelligent, confident, capable women in film and television; this has done only so much to revolutionize the category of gender itself. This is why theory must change with the historical moments that theory itself worked so tirelessly to transform. If, as I have argued, where there is a shift in mode of production there is a relegation to the primal psychoanalytic scene with its concomitant gender oppression, then it is more imperative than ever to examine this phenomenon in the period of late capitalism, which is above all a shift in production from, in the United States, a manufacturing society to an information one. How might gender be used to foreclose on meaningful political discussion during this shift? Will things necessarily be better for women once capitalism ends? This essay suggests the urgency of this question.

Notes

1. Zizek draws a distinction between the cynic and the ironist in their relation to the symbolic order: "from the right premise that 'the big Other doesn't exist,' i.e. that the symbolic order is a fiction, the cynicist draws the wrong conclusion that the big Other doesn't 'function,' that its role can simply be discounted – due to his failure to notice how the symbolic fiction nonetheless regulates his relationship to

the real of enjoyment, he remains all the more enslaved to the symbolic context that defines his access to the Thing-Enjoyment, caught in the symbolic ritual he publicly mocks. This, preciely, is what Lacan has in mind with his *les non-dupes errent*: those who are not duped by the symbolic fiction are most deeply in error. The ironist's apparently 'softer' approach, on the other hand, far more effectively unbinds the nodal points that hold together the symbolic universe, i.e. it is the ironist who effectively assumes the non-existence of the Other" ("Joyce-the-Symptom").

2. These intersecting points are, in Lacan's register, *points de capiton*.

3. Since Duchovny's departure from *The X Files*, he has appeared in several poorly rated films, proving the ultimate total dependence *he* had on the series. His megalomaniacal restlessness proved to be his downfall. Moreover, like capitalism, it was in his nature to destroy, in an attempt to increase profit, that which engendered his success.

Works Cited

Eagleton, Terry. *After Theory*. New York: Basic Books, 2003.

Freud, Sigmund. *Dora: An Analysis of a Case of Hysteria*. Ed. Philip Rieff. New York: Macmillan, 1963.

---. *The Standard Edition of the Complete Psychological Works of Sigmund Freud*. Trans. James Strachey. Vol. XII (1911-1913), London: Hogarth, 1958.

Jameson, Fredric. Foreword. *The Postmodern Condition: A Report of Knowledge*. By Francois Lyotard. Manchester, UK: Manchester UP, 1984. vii-xxii.

Lacan, Jacques. *Écrits: A Selection*. Trans. Alan Sheridan. New York: W.W. Norton, 1977.

---. *The Ethics of Psychoanalysis: The Seminar of Jacques Lacan Book VII, 1959-1960*. Ed. Jacques-Alain Miller. Trans. Dennis Porter. New York: W.W. Norton, 1986.

Lyotard, Francois. *The Postmodern Condition: A Report of Knowledge*. Manchester, UK: Manchester UP, 1984.

Marcuse, Herbert, Robert Paul Wolff, and Barrington Moore, Jr. *A Critique of Pure Tolerance*. Boston: Beacon Press, 1965.

Wood, Ellen. *Empire of Capital*. London and New York: Verso, 2003.

The X Files. Dir. Rob Bowman. Twentieth Century Fox, 1998.

Zizek, Slavoj. *Looking Awry: An Introduction to Jacques Lacan through Popular Culture*. Cambridge: MIT P, 1991.

---. "From Joyce-the-Symptom." *Lacanian Ink* 11(1997): http://www.lacan.com/frameXI2.htm

20

2

"Enchanted Island":
Hawaii, and Other American Fantasies

Brian Ireland

Western explorers and adventurers such as Captain James Cook, William Ellis, and Charles Stewart, returned from the Pacific with exciting "South Seas" tales of Eden-like islands, idol-worshipping natives, man-eating cannibals, lost treasure, and beautiful, available native women. Novelists such as Herman Melville, Mark Twain, Robert Louis Stevenson, and Henry de Vere Stacpoole would later add elements to the mythology in their semi-fictional tales. By the time Hollywood started making movies about the South Seas in the early years of the twentieth century, there was already familiar, exotic imagery to draw upon – recurring plot devices that were evident in the stories of earlier adventurers and novelists, with themes of mystery, romance, danger, adventure, opportunity, and utopianism. As recent scholarship has shown, Westerners have created, in all of these mediums, semi-mythical places, whose inhabitants reflect Western desires and prejudices (see especially Obeyesekere, Wood, and Desmond).

One particular island chain and its inhabitants have suffered badly from these Western fantasies, and that is Hawaii. "Discovered" in 1778 by Captain James Cook, Hawaii was ravaged by Western diseases and rapidly depopulated from perhaps 800,000-1,000,000 Native Hawaiians in 1778 to as little as 40,000 by the mid-nineteenth century. This depopulation and concurrent social disruption, together with foreign interference in the culture, economy, and politics of Native Hawaiians, led to loss of indigenous sovereignty in 1898, when the formerly independent Kingdom of Hawaii was incorporated by the United States. Foreign influence in Hawaii has had devastating consequences for the Hawaiian people, and over 100 years of American rule has not given Native Hawaiians the promised "American Dream." In fact, as Native Hawaiian activist and scholar Haunani-Kay Trask states, Native Hawaiians are "a politically subordinated group suffering all the legacies of conquest: landlessness, disastrous health, diaspora, institutionalization in the military and prisons, poor educational attainment, and confinement to the service sector of employment" ("Settlers of Color" 3).

Despite this, the common image Westerners have of Hawaii is that of an island paradise, a feminized, welcoming place of leisure and libido. University of Hawaii professors Kathy Ferguson and Phyllis Turnbull argue that this visualization of Hawaii is a creation of the Western imagination. They state:

> Western intrusions into Hawaii – from early explorers, traders, and missionaries, to planters, diplomats, and military leaders, to travel agents, airline companies, and foreign visitors – have seen Hawaii as a welcoming feminine place, waiting with open arms to embrace those who come to penetrate, protect, mold, and develop, while simultaneously lacking that which would make it fully realized (and which the intruders conveniently believe themselves to possess). Maps of Hawaii from Captain James Cook's expeditions represent Hawaii with soft, curved, breast-like mountains and mysterious coves and bays.... Missionary accounts of "the natives" emphasize their darkness; naked, unashamed, promiscuous. (*Oh, Say, Can You See?* 6)

The "other Hawaii" discussed here is one that is both masked by and depends on the collected memory of December 7, 1941, the Japanese attack on Pearl Harbor. Hawaii is, today, home to one of the largest military arsenals in the world. It is a vital American strategic possession, and it holds the dubious distinction of being the most heavily militarized state in the United States. The U.S. military owns or uses twenty-five percent of the land on the island of Oahu alone. In addition to 112,000 military veterans who have settled in Hawaii, there are 78,346 active military personnel who, with their dependants, comprise almost seven percent of the population (Schmitt, *Hawaii Data Book* 1). Hawaii today is the home of the U.S. Pacific Command, which has been described as "the largest unified military operation in the world" (Albertini, Foster, Inglis, and Roeder 2). Based in Hawaii are Polaris and Poseidon nuclear submarines, the Fifth and Seventh U.S. Fleets, large amounts of personnel and equipment at Schofield Barracks, Tripler Army Medical Center, Hickham Air Force Base, Wheeler Air Force Base, Kaneohe Bay Marine Corps Air Station, and various other military installations, tracking facilities, radar posts, training grounds, firing ranges, and research facilities. The military owns or controls vast swathes of fertile land, including training grounds at Pohakuloa and Kawailoa totaling 161,000 acres (Albertini et al. 7). In addition, the island of Kauai is the home of the U.S. military's Pacific Missile Test Range Station at Barking Sands, established in 1966.

There is much liminal space between these two contrasting images of Hawaii and numerous narrative crossover points. While scholars have examined both areas individually, no attempt has been made to join the two parts together – to use a cohesive, holistic, approach to examine, for example, exactly what part Hawaii plays in the American national consciousness. Is Hawaii a "paradise of the Pacific," a militarized "Gibraltar of the Pacific," or some combination of both? How did the Pearl Harbor attack affect America's view of Hawaii, and what part did Hollywood play in shaping that view? University of Hawaii professor Floyd Matson states, "To people who live anywhere else, as we know, Hawaii is a state of mind. But it is not always the same state of mind.... [T]here is doubtless a kind of 'monomyth' at the heart of the matter – one which has much to do with islands but little to do with *these* islands" (40). As Matson notes, the reality of Hawaii, and the Hawaii that exists in the American mind, are two separate entities.

There is no other medium that best illustrates America's imaginary Hawaii than Hollywood movies. Houston Wood argues that "most of what Euroamericans today know about Hawaii they have learned from movies and television" (103). Hawaii and Hawaiians have been shaped and reshaped by Hollywood to meet the needs and expectations of a mainland American audience, just as the New World and Native Americans were invented then reinvented by European colonizers to meet their needs. Journalist and author Tom Engelhardt refers to this "invented" aspect of the conquest of America as the "American war story," a narrative that acts as a "builder of national consciousness" (5). Engelhardt's analysis of this "war story" in a wide range of historical and cultural artifacts and productions, offers a useful framework for analyzing Hawaii's role in the war story and in the American national consciousness. It is particularly valuable for examining movies, since his analysis deals with the link between political decision-making and the stories we tell about the past and about other peoples, which influence those decisions.[1]

Engelhardt argues that the American national narrative is based on war stories about "savage," uncivilized Indians and "peaceful" civilized settlers. Stories Americans tell about their past reverse the role of invader and invaded, and offer a comfortable historical narrative that is free from unsettling themes such as genocide, colonialism, and imperialism. Political scientist and media commentator Michael Parenti maintains that in television and movies, "The homeland, the safe place, is American White Anglo-Protestant, or at least White. It is inhabited by people who are sane and care about life. The enemies are maniacal and careless with lives, including their own" (14). In cowboy films, for example, the intruder changes places with the intruded upon when Indians are shown attacking forts, wagon trains, and homes. Seldom do these movies portray Westerners attacking Indian homes and villages because, as is evident in movies such as *Little Big Man* (1970) and *Soldier Blue* (1970), such images remind viewers that they are the descendants of intruders and invaders. Furthermore, the savagery of the ambushes and "sneak" attacks on supposedly civilized settlers acts as an excuse for the terrible retribution that will inevitably be inflicted on the "savages." Engelhardt states, "From its origins, the war story was essentially defensive in nature.... [I]t was the Indians who, by the ambush, the atrocity, and the capture of the white women...became the aggressors, and so sealed their own fate" (5).

Hollywood portrayals of Hawaii have changed throughout the twentieth century to meet the requirements of American movie audiences. Although some stereotypes and themes are present throughout, three distinct phases can be detected. Before World War II, Hawaii and its people were portrayed as exotically different from America; after World War II, Hollywood movies still portrayed Hawaii as exotic, but in various ways Hawaii is made to seem similar to, or connected to the rest of the United States; and from the mid-1950s through the 1960s, "American Hawaii" was displayed as a racial paradigm, an example the troubled mainland ought to follow. In each distinct period, Hawaii is shaped according to the needs of the mainland American audience.

Pre-World War II Hawaii movie titles emphasize difference, such as non-American exotic locations, animals, phrases or practices. Some examples of this are *The Shark God* (1913), *Martin Eden* (1914), *Aloha Oe* (1915), *Kaolulolani* (1916), *The Island of Desire* (1917), *The Bottle Imp* (1917), *The Hidden Pearls* (1918), *A Fallen Idol* (1919), *Passion Fruit*

(1921), *Hula* (1927), *The Chinese Parrot* (1927), *The Kamaaina* (1929), *Aloha* (1931), *Bird of Paradise* (1932), *China Clipper* (1936), *Trade Winds* (1939), *Karayo* (1940), and *South of Pago Pago* (1940). In contrast, post-Pearl Harbor movies that feature Hawaii have non-exotic names that are often connected to the U.S. military, such as *Air Force* (1943), *Million Dollar Weekend* (1948), *Miss Tatlock's Millions* (1948), *The Big Lift* (1950), *Go For Broke* (1951), *Sailor Beware* (1952), *Big Jim McLain* (1952), *From Here To Eternity* (1953), *Miss Sadie Thompson* (1954), *Beachhead* (1954), *Hell's Half Acre* (1954), *The High And The Mighty* (1954), *Mister Roberts* (1955), and *The Revolt Of Mamie Stover* (1956).

Pre-Pearl Harbor movies also tend to have specific Hawaii or Hawaiian place names in their titles. In the pre-war years, such titles evoked images of an idyllic island paradise that mainland Americans could escape to for the price of a ticket at their local cinema. Examples includes *Hawaiian Love* (1913), *It Happened To Honolulu* (1916), *Happy Hawaii* (1928), *Waikiki Wedding* (1937), *Wings Over Honolulu* (1937), *Hawaii Calls* (1938), *Hawaiian Buckaroo* (1938), *Charlie Chan in Honolulu* (1938), *Honolulu* (1939), *Hawaiian Nights* (1939), *Moonlight in Hawaii* (1941), and *Honolulu Lu* (1941). In contrast, between 1942 and 1956 only one movie – *Ma and Pa Kettle in Waikiki* – has a Hawaii place name in its title. This may reflect a change in how mainland Americans thought about Hawaii. In the post-Pearl Harbor years, Americans no longer considered Hawaii as a place apart from the rest of the country. While it was still a distant territory, geographically and politically, the Japanese attack had foregrounded Hawaii in America's national consciousness.

Americans have traditionally imagined Hawaii and other "South Seas" islands as places of restful relaxation away from the rigors of life on the mainland United States. These islands are places where the "normal" rules of behavior do not apply. Hollywood movies have played a large role in creating this enduring myth of an uninhibited island paradise and the conventions of the genre rarely reflect the reality of Hawaii and its people. For example, *Bird of Paradise* (1951) was filmed in Hawaii and features Hawaiian language and the Hawaiian god, Pele (Wood 1). Its plot is sensationalist and derivative: Frenchman Andre (Louis Jourdan) is shocked and disgusted when his otherwise demure Polynesian girlfriend Kalua (Debra Paget) throws herself into a volcano as a sacrifice to a pagan god (Reyes and Rampell 65). In movies such as *The Idol Dancer* (1920) and *Mutiny on the Bounty* (1962), lascivious native women are willing to share their bodies with white explorers or seamen. Audiences are often told, in "South Seas" movies, that natives consider European explorers as "gods," and what primitive woman would not want to please her god?

Haunani-Kay Trask insists that for Americans, Hawaii is "[m]ostly a state of mind...[t]his fictional Hawaii comes out of the depths of Western sexual sickness that demands a dark, sin-free native for instant gratification." The image and attraction of Hawaii, Trask believes, comes in part from "slick Hollywood movies" (*From a Native Daughter* 136-7). In the early years of film, Hawaii was depicted as being different from, or "other" than the United States. Hawaii was exotic, primitive, and dangerous. Common themes that emphasize these differences include plots about volcanoes, savage and perhaps man-eating natives, sexually available native women, explicit displays of licentiousness, strange social customs, and pagan religious practices. In movies such as *Aloha Oe* (1915) and *A Fallen Idol* (1919), the leading native ladies are royals (Wood 113), a reminder that Hawaii was different, feudal, and anachronistic. In as much as their budget would allow it, many of these movies linger on the beautiful, exotic landscapes of Hawaii and other Pacific islands, another factor that emphasizes difference from America. Historian Robert Schmitt states, for example, that, "At least 11 of the pictures made in or about Hawaii featured volcanoes, either real...or fictional. Most of these volcanoes were filmed in fiery eruption...threatening either to claim the heroine, overrun a village, or even blow up an entire island. One Hawaii-made movie, *South of Pago Pago*, contained a smoking volcano that did not erupt, to the astonishment of several reviewers" (*Hawaii in the Movies* 5). Schmitt's study of Hawaii movies that were released between 1898 and 1959 illustrates that ten out of eleven "volcano movies" were made before Pearl Harbor, out of a total of seventy-five movies made between 1898 and 1941 inclusively. In contrast, after Pearl Harbor only one was released (*Bird of Paradise*).

Like the tourist literature of the period, Hawaii was deliberately marketed as a place where the sexual rules of American society were either relaxed or completely absent. Hollywood relied on blatant sexual stereotyping of native women to emphasize this difference. Westerners directly associated the physical racial characteristics of native women with this supposed sexual wantonness. Even today, as University of Iowa professor Jane Desmond notes, tourists expect hula dancers to be young, slender, attractive, dark-skinned, longhaired brunettes. This look, Desmond affirms, "communicate[s] the notion of 'Hawaii' as different from the United States" (135). Native women are, according to these movie scripts, unlike the supposedly chaste and "civilized" American women of the time. In contrast to these reserved females, native women are alluring and sexually available. The occasional filmmaker who threatened this stereotype was met with industry and audience disapproval. For example, when Robert Flaherty was tasked by Paramount to go to Samoa to make a similar documentary to his successful *Nanook of the North* (1922), his resulting work, *Moana* (1926), proved to be a disappointment to the studio, as it portrayed none of the stereotypical images that American audiences had come to expect. As film critics Thomas and Vivian Sobchack point out, "In commercial desperation, Paramount misguidedly advertised the film as 'the love life of a South Sea siren' and the film, not delivering what it promised, proved to be a box office flop" (344).

Hollywood perpetuated the image of Hawaii in particular as a peaceful, romantic paradise. In *Honolulu*, for example, actor Robert Young states, "I'd like to go to Hawaii. It's quiet and peaceful there." His co-star, actress Gracie Allen, sings, "I know it's gonna be, a great big blow to me, unless I find romance in Honolulu." The 1927 film *Hula* features Clara Bow as an "unconquered island girl who comes face to face with love!" (Schmitt, *Hawaii in the Movies* 29). In *Tin Pan Alley* (1940), actresses Alice Faye and Betty Grable sing, "Hawaii, a lovely Hawaii. It's like Heaven on the blue Pacific shore. Oh won't you let me go-a, to the land of sweet aloha, won't you let me linger there forever more."

To a large extent, American audiences of that time period simply imposed mainland racial attitudes onto Hawaiian society. Yet, the idea that Hawaii was poly-racial also served to remind those mainland audiences how different Hawaii really was. For example, *Bird of Paradise* (1932) is based on a 1912 Broadway musical by Richard W. Tully, which historian DeSoto Brown describes as "deeply offensive racism." For example, one white character states that he "kept his soul, his white soul, pure from contamination with the brown race." The musical also features "the phony concept of human sacrifices leaping into hot lava" (6). *Bird of Paradise* begins with a dramatic scene in which a native girl (Dolores Del Rio) saves a white sailor from a predatory shark. Immediately, we see the stereotypical images of both the danger and romance of "The Islands." Like the 1952 remake, this version of *Bird of Paradise* features a ludicrous volcano sacrifice scene that reminds viewers of the primitive, barbaric, and thoroughly *un-American* nature of the natives.

Although these are, for the most part, artistically inconsequential films, visual images conveyed to large groups of viewers can create powerful and enduring mythologies. Both *Flirtation Walk* (1934) and *Waikiki Wedding* were released in the aftermath of infamous and racially inflammatory crime cases. In 1928, for example, Myles Fukunaga, a Japanese man, abducted and murdered a 10-year-old *haole* (white) boy called Gill Jamieson, a crime for which he was subsequently executed. Furthermore, in 1931, Navy wife Thalia Massie accused five local men of raping her. The subsequent trial sparked a racial controversy and eventually led to the kidnapping and murder of one of the five accused by Massie's husband, mother, and a U.S. naval seaman. While audiences today may laugh at such portrayals of gangs of threatening Hawaiians in vintage movies, in the late 1930s these scenes would have resonated strongly with mainland audiences, reminding them of the supposedly dangerous and primitive circumstances that white settlers faced living amongst "natives."

Hawaii Calls (1938) begins in San Francisco, with shots of passengers boarding a cruise ship, and the ship sailing out under Golden Gate Bridge. The effect of this is to remind viewers that to get to Hawaii they must first leave America and then travel by ship for days to reach this foreign destination. As one character states, their destination is more a state of mind than an actual place: "Honolulu, Waikiki, bananas, pineapple, hula dancers [and] sunshine." This exotic imagery is reinforced when the ship arrives in Honolulu and dozens of native boys swim alongside waiting for passengers to throw money overboard. Two young stowaways, *haole* Billy Coulter (Bobby Breen) and Native Hawaiian Pua (Pua Lani), dive into the water to join the other boys. Billy is, in effect, "going native" in emulating his friend's athletic feat. On the run from the ship's Captain and the law, the two boys are taken in by a Native Hawaiian lady named Hina (Mamo Clark). Again, to emphasize cultural difference, every native speaks Hawaiian when they are with their own cultural group whereas haoles speak only English.

The plot of *Hawaii Calls*, such as it is, centers on a plot to steal U.S. Naval officer Commander Milburn's secret plans that are "valuable to the safety of the Hawaiian Islands." A German spy named Muller recruits local criminal elements like Julius, a Japanese driver and servant for Milburn's fiancé's family. This plotline has all the military excuses for American involvement in Hawaii, namely the internal and external threat of disloyal Japanese and a concerted effort on behalf of "foreign" Axis powers to obtain plans for the defense of Hawaii. When Julius, a long-time servant to the Millburns, "betrays" his colonial masters by stealing the secret plans, the movie asks the audience to gaze not in the direction of the obviously incompetent Milburn or at the wisdom of sending supposedly top secret plans with a lone naval officer on a civilian cruise ship, but instead at the disloyalty and treachery of the previously trusted Japanese man – a metaphor for the overall situation of the Japanese in Hawaii and their relationship with America. The end of the movie relieves the audience, however: with the help of Billy, the conspirators are discovered and shot to death by police.

A sub-theme of *Hawaii Calls* is concern by the Americans for the welfare of Billy in Hawaii. He is, as the audience has been reminded on a number of occasions, a white boy who is in danger of going native. Billy himself is aware of this fact, in that he asks Milburn if he is "disappointed" in his behavior. Milburn tells him, "Captain O'Hare says he wouldn't be surprised if you went back [to the United States] of your own accord." The movie's message is that Hawaii is a good place for a vacation, is strategically significant and therefore needs the "protection" of the United States military, but is also filled with dangerous foreigners and criminal elements. Although he is an orphan, Billy is still cultured: he sings beautiful songs throughout and is mindful of his manners. In contrast, Pua lives with an extended Hawaiian family and yet is almost feral in nature. Obviously, therefore, Hawaii is no place for a Caucasian boy. As he leaves the islands on O'Hare's ship, Billy, now dressed in a miniature navy uniform, sings "Aloha Oe." Ashore, Pua and Hina bid him a tearful farewell as he heads home to America, the homeland, the place *Hawaii Calls* tells us, where he really belongs.

Honolulu features a Chinese man in a prominent role, Smith's servant, Wong (Willie Fung). According to *Variety*, however, Wong provides only "brief but hilarious contributions" in a stereotypical role where the audience is asked to laugh at the "foreigner" who speaks such broken English as "me know, me know." *Honolulu* makes full use of the image of Hawaii as a paradise by showing many "outdoor" scenes, even if they were shot on a soundstage. For example, one scene features a waterfall, at the base of which is a *luau* (feast) featuring a circle of Hawaiian and *haole* diners. Native Hawaiian dancers, singers, and musicians entertain this group. The scenes remind viewers that Hawaii contains people, customs, and scenery that are not American. *Honolulu* is so bad, according to the *New York Times* review, "if things are the way the picture makes out [Hawaii] should be freed before the Philippines" (1580-1581). A comment such as this would be near impossible in the post-Pearl Harbor world.

Before World War II, Hawaii was a marginal part of the United States. Leila Reiplinger, a Hawaiian hula dancer who travelled to New York in 1940, recalls, for example, a history teacher who thought, "we were still the Sandwich Islands" (qtd. in Desmond 108). In contrast, a post-Pearl Harbor 1942 article in *Asia Magazine* referred to the Hawaii as "American Hawaii" (qtd. in Desmond 119). Authors Beth Bailey and David Farber state, "Hawaii is about as far from 'representative' as one can get in 1940s America. Hawaii was at the margin of American life as well as of the war" (19). No single incident would change the course of American history in the twentieth century more than the Japanese attack on Pearl Harbor on December 7th, 1941. Almost 2,500 U.S. servicemen and civilians were killed and a severe blow dealt to U.S. military and national prestige. The attack would have wide-reaching effects on life in Hawaii, but it would also affect change in Hollywood and the "South Seas" genre of film.

After the attack on Pearl Harbor, many Hollywood movies about Hawaii served to further this aim of Americanization. They did this by eliminating Native Hawaiians from the screen, replacing them with an almost all-white cast, and emphasizing the normality of everyday American life in the islands. Even the titles of movies about Hawaii changed: before the war many movies had titles with colors in them, perhaps to emphasize racial differences between white and black, and to suggest the possibility of forbidden interracial liaisons. Jane Desmond notes that between 1920 and 1939, "more than fifty feature films were made in or about Hawaii. A genre of South Seas island romance was particularly popular, often featuring interracial romance between native women and Caucasian men (businessmen, shipwreck victims) visiting the islands" (109). Some examples of movies with color-laden titles are *The Black Lili* (1921), *The White Flower* (1923), *Beware of Blondes* (1928), *The Black Camel* (1931), *The Blonde Captive* (1931), *White Heat* (1934), and *Mutiny on the Blackhawk* (1939). In contrast, not one movie listed in Robert Schmitt's *Hawaii in the Movies* that was made after Pearl Harbor has a color in the title.

The exotic locales of pre-war movies were replaced, for a time, in post-Pearl Harbor movies with backdrops of military bases, built-up urban areas, factories, shipyards, yacht clubs, city scenes, and modern technology. For example, the 1956 movie *The Revolt of Mamie Stover* does not focus on palm trees, beaches, or the scenic majesty of Diamond Head. Instead, it tells the seedy story of a Honolulu prostitute. Most of the action in that movie takes place indoors, at a nightclub, a residential home, or in restaurants or hotels. One scene is set on a golf course and country club. Similarly, *From Here To Eternity* chooses, with one notable exception, not to feature exotic locales and instead focuses on indoor scenes at Schofield Barracks or at River Street brothels.

Pre-Pearl Harbor movies emphasize how different the United States was to the supposedly exotic, primitive, and dangerous Hawaiian Islands. They achieve this by frequent use of recurring thematic elements and visual reminders, including an emphasis on nature, wildlife and landscape, plots about volcanoes, savage natives, cannibalism, sexually obtainable native women, explicit displays of nudity and passion, odd social customs, and pagan religious rites. In the years after Pearl Harbor, however, Hollywood movies served to remind mainland Americans that Hawaii was part of the United States, as American as apple pie and baseball. Hollywood may have been responding to changing audience expectations – assuaging the American "feel good" factor. For example, the Japanese attack on Pearl Harbor led to such vicious retaliation by the United States that many commentators and historians view the war in the Pacific as being essentially different to the war in Europe. John Dower points to the racial nature of propaganda and newspaper coverage as evidence that Americans viewed the Japanese as vicious, subhuman savages, and that the Pearl Harbor attack released "emotions forgotten since our most savage Indian wars were awakened by the ferocities of the Japanese commanders" (33). American audiences needed to feel that such ferocity was justified: no one wants to be seen as a racist, after all, and no one wanted to be reminded of the American colonization of Hawaii. Therefore, if Americans convinced themselves that they were the innocent party, that *they* were attacked at Pearl Harbor, and that the attack was more perfidious in nature than simply two colonial armies tussling over their governments' colonial possessions in the Pacific, then attention could be drawn away from the racist nature of the retaliation and from the fact that the Japanese attacked only military targets on the "American Gibraltar."

In Hollywood movies, Hawaii's Americanization was achieved through subtle changes in recurring themes and imagery, and also by omission. Pre-war movies usually featured native village activities such as feasts, ceremonies, religious practices etc. These social customs emphasized how different native society was compared to Western. However, as Houston Wood notes, at the beginning of World War II, "Native village life all but disappear[s], a tropological development that reaches its contemporary form in the Elvis films of the 1960s" (117). Whereas exotic and sometimes threatening native men, dressed usually in native attire, played major roles in early Hawaii films, in post-Pearl Harbor movies such masculine native exoticism disappears from the screen. There is no post-Pearl Harbor equivalent of Duke Kahanamoku, for example, who features in many early Hollywood films and television shows (Brennan).[2] In most of these movies, Hawaiians are either entirely absent, or they play small roles as waiters, barmen, or musicians. In *From Here to Eternity*, for example, the only Hawaiians on view are servants, waiters, and entertainers, all of whom are dressed in non-native apparel or non-threatening aloha shirts.

Americanization in Hollywood movies also operates by focusing less on nature and landscapes and more on urban and industrial Hawaii, or on the U.S. military. For example, ten pre-Pearl Harbor movies about Hawaii had military themes – *Excuse Me* (1925), *The Non-Stop Flight* (1926), *The Flying Fleet* (1929), *Leathernecking* (1930), *Flirtation Walk* (1934), *Navy Wife* (1935), *Wings Over Honolulu* (1937), *Dive Bomber* (1941), *Navy Blues* (1941) and *In the Navy* (1941). In contrast, and for obvious reasons, many post-Pearl Harbor movies feature war or military themes. These include *Submarine Raider* (1942), *Air Force* (1943), *December 7* (1943), *On an Island With You* (1948), *Task Force* (1949), *Sands of Iwo Jima* (1949), *The Big Lift* (1950) *Operation Pacific* (1951), *Go For Broke!* (1951), *Sailor Beware* (1952), *From Here To Eternity* (1953), *The Caine Mutiny* (1954), *The Revolt of Mamie Stover* (1956), *The Lieutenant Wore Skirts* (1956), *Away All Boats* (1956), *Jungle Heat* (1957), *Torpedo Run* (1958), *The Gallant Hours* (1960), *In Harm's Way* (1965), *Tora! Tora! Tora!* (1970), *Midway* (1976), and *Pearl Harbor* (2001).

Not only do these movies focus on Americans and American culture and divest Hawaii of Native Hawaiians and their culture, many of them also perpetuate myths about the Japanese attack on Pearl Harbor that serve to make the Japanese look savage, devious, and barbaric. Engelhardt states, "At the heart of the war story lay the ambush, extraordinary evidence of the enemy's treacherous behavior. While all ambushes involved deceit, none was more heinous than the 'sneak attack,' that surprise assault on a peaceful, unsuspecting people" (39). Such "sneak attacks" occur in movies like *Submarine Raider, December 7, The Final Countdown* (1980), and *Pearl Harbor*, in which civilians are attacked as well as military targets. In fact, much if not all of the damage caused to the city of Honolulu was a result of spent U.S. Navy shells that had been fired into the air and had then fallen on civilian areas. For example, an explosion at the Governor's mansion that killed one civilian was actually caused by a Navy five-inch anti-aircraft shell (Editors of the Army Times 101).

In the movies, however, showing historically incorrect attacks on U.S. civilians perpetuates the image of the Japanese as devious and savage. In *Submarine Raider*, for example, an American woman "survives the shelling of her luxury yacht in Hawaiian waters by a Japanese aircraft carrier," and a Federal agent fights "suspected spies and saboteurs in the Islands" (Reyes and Rampell 15). In *Task Force*, Japanese warplanes attack three American women playing tennis. *In Harm's Way* contains a scene in which a Japanese plane attacks a civilian couple on a beach. In *Pearl Harbor*, a Japanese pilot attacks a civilian convertible car. In John Ford's documentary *December 7*, Japanese citizens in Hawaii spy on the U.S. fleet and report back to the Japanese embassy. When the Japanese finally attack in *December 7*, warplanes strike civilian targets as well as military. The movie *Air Force* "claims there were Japanese snipers on Maui and that Japanese vegetable trucks from Honolulu smashed into the planes at Hickam Field" (Reyes and Rampell 11). The plot of *Jungle Heat* involves labor disputes and Japanese spies on Kauai, where, according to Schmitt, "war veterans' groups strongly objected to its portrayal of disloyalty among Japanese residents" (*Hawaii in the Movies* 71).

These movies dehumanize the Japanese and paint them as totally immoral, deviant, underhanded, and barbaric. Engelhardt states, "The Japanese attack on Pearl Harbor fit the lineaments of this [war] story well. At the country's periphery, a savage, nonwhite enemy had launched a barbaric attack on Americans going about their lives early one Sunday morning" (5). Clearly, Hollywood was determined to play its part in forming this narrative, and now we see in hindsight that such misinformation and propaganda had the desired effect: the *New York Times* review notes, for example, that a 1942 theater audience for *Submarine Raider* "was in fine hissing form" at the movie's "scrupulously fair...portrayal of the enemy" (1874).

Engelhardt notes in the war story that when a savage enemy massacres Americans, rumors often spread that either traitorous Americans were involved, or perhaps, the savage enemy was part European in heritage. After all, what else could explain how and why savages could defeat a civilized people? Thus, when Custer's Indian killers were defeated in 1876, rumor spread that white men dressed as Indians were leading the attack, or that Sitting Bull was a "half-breed" Frenchman. Engelhardt notes that when General Douglas MacArthur heard the news that his air force in the Philippines had been destroyed from the air, he "refused to believe that the pilots could've been Japanese. He insisted they must have been white mercenaries" (39). Historian Paul Fussell points out that in any war, "one's defeats and disasters are caused by treasonous traffic with the enemy rather than by one's own blundering amateurism is always a popular idea" (39-40).

In *December 7* (1943), by careful framing, editing, and special effects, director John Ford creates images of the Japanese in Hawaii as insect-like hordes threatening to overrun the outnumbered American population. For example, he uses montage, quick editing, and fast-paced music to suggest the ant-like Japanese are overwhelming whites. Furthermore, Ford uses frequent close-ups of Japanese as a reminder of physical racial otherness. A Japanese official is shown as a bowing, grinning fool, for example. Also, Japanese kids are shown singing "God Bless America," but the narrator says there is "a hyphenated loyalty." The first eighty-three minute length version of *December 7* was banned by the War Department because, in the commonly-accepted version of events, the U.S. military objected to portrayals of its ineptitude. However, an Oscar-winning thirty minute version of the documentary, without references to racial differences and Japanese espionage, was eventually released in 1943. It is possible that it was the original version of *December 7*'s portrayal of Hawaii as a unique place, quite unlike the United States, that U.S. authorities objected to. Such a depiction would have reminded wartime American audiences that Hawaii was, in essence, a U.S. colony and may have called into question the scope and extent of American retaliation.

Recurring thematic elements and visual images of early Hollywood movies about Hawaii or the South Seas emphasize the exotic and primitive otherness of islands. In contrast, films such as *From Here To Eternity*, *The Revolt of Mamie Stover*, and *Big Jim McLain* de-emphasized such otherness by ignoring familiar plot devices about volcanoes, savage natives, and cannibalism. Furthermore, post-Pearl Harbor movies tend to show urban rather than rural life, in contrast to earlier movies that focus on themes of nature, wildlife and landscape. Gone too were Hawaiians with their "odd" social customs, strange language, and pagan religious rites. Instead, we have plots that focus on Americans and the Americanization of Hawaii in areas such as technology, politics, culture, and the military.

Like no other movie, *Big Jim McLain*, starring John Wayne, attempts to "Americanize" Hawaii. Wayne is more than a bit-part player in Engelhardt's war story, as cultural historian Gary Wills tangentially notes:

> John Ford had come out of World War II in love with the Navy, with military units in general, and with America's new imperial role in the world as the asserter of freedom everywhere. The three "Seventh Cavalry" films he made with Wayne from 1948 to 1950 reflect this attitude, and put Wayne at the center of Cold War sensibility striving for social discipline in time of trial. In 1949, the Soviets exploded their first atom bomb and Communists won their war for China. In 1950, President Truman escalated the nuclear competition by deciding to create the hydrogen bomb. The image of cavalry units surrounded by hostile Indians echoed the fears of Americans trying to remain steady as peril increased. Wayne became the cool but determined model for Americans living with continual danger. (Wills 147)

Big Jim McLain (1952) is a documentary-style work of anti-communist propaganda in the same vein as other "anti-Red" movies as *The Red Menace* (1949), *I Married a Communist* (1950), and *I Was a Communist for the FBI* (1951). This documentary technique adds weight to a flimsy script and authority to otherwise laughable portrayals of supposed communists who, Wills notes, "abjure smiles [and] cannot speak without sneering" (Wills 184). Wayne (whose character shares initials with Senator Joseph McCarthy) is an investigator for the House Committee on Un-American Activities who is sent to Hawaii to find communist agitators. A younger, impetuous sidekick called Mal Baxter (James Arness) accompanies him. The film has a see-through plot, cardboard characters, and poor acting. However, it is notable for the way in which it transforms earlier movie images of Hawaii as different and exotic into a Hawaii that is loyally American.

Wayne's villains are untypical of earlier Hawaii movies. In those early movies, criminals and rogues are typically either natives or of mixed race. In *Big Jim McLain*, however, the villains are mostly Caucasians. In other words, they are un-American because they are communists, not because of their skin color or racial origin. This reflected a new Cold War trend in filmmaking that played off fears of "reds under the bed," the McCarthy hearings, blacklists, and paranoia about foreigners. These villains are involved in a plot to disrupt shipping and stop supplies to U.S. troops fighting the Korean War. Their methods are both modern and devious: they plan to use not only labor disputes, but also bacteriological warfare spread by rats. Such imagery could only remind the viewing audience of earlier dehumanizing propaganda about the Japanese. The plot utilized irrational fears about labor unions such as the International Longshoremen's and Warehousemen's Union, and economic strikes such as the sugar workers' strike of 1946, a pineapple workers' strike of 1947, and an ILWU strike of 1949.[3] Wayne's mission was to find who or what was un-American, and to eliminate it, thus drawing Hawaii even closer into the American fold.

The movie opposes earlier stereotypes about Hawaii as backward and rural. For example, unlike previous movies in which travelers arrive on ships and alight at the Aloha Tower dock, Wayne travels in a state of the art commercial jet and arrives at the newly built Honolulu International Airport. There are no native urchins on view begging for coins as in *Hawaii Calls*. Instead, there are carefully orchestrated hula girls to welcome tourists with *leis*. When Wayne and Baxter arrive at their duplex, Baxter displays more modern technology when he sets up a listening device to spy on the occupants of the next apartment. That the occupants are honeymooners adds to the well-worn theme of titillation and male-gaze voyeurism of this genre of movies. However, Wayne's comment to Baxter, "Who do you think we're working for – Dr. Kinsey," adds to the modern "cutting edge" feel of the movie. Later, we are told that the contents of a suspect's luggage are "microscopically photographed," and that "security agencies have been listening to some very interesting conversations." This information not only conveys that the security services are on top of the communist problem, but also illustrates that all the modern technological resources of America in the 1950s are also available in Hawaii.

Unlike earlier films, evident in *Big Jim McLain* are a contemporary, tiled hospital, a psychiatric hospital, a modern doctor's office, and the clean, tourist-filled Royal Hawaiian Hotel. Instead of the native outrigger canoes of *Mutiny on the Bounty* and many other early movies, in *Big Jim McLain* we have scenes set at the Outrigger Canoe Club, where modern American yachts predominate. Furthermore, in mentioning that she "attends a course of lectures at the university on Saturdays," Wayne's love interest, Nancy Olson (actress Nancy Vallon) subtly reminds the audience that Hawaii is no longer the culturally "backward" island of earlier movies and is now a modern, sophisticated state like any other.

Like no other film before or since, *Big Jim McLain* reverses the role of invader or colonist and native. A prime example of this is the movie's portrayal of the Honolulu Police Department, which is very different to how the HPD was viewed before World War II. For example, in the 1930s during the infamous Massie rape case, island haoles, the military, the mainland newspaper, and political interests criticized the Honolulu Police Department as corrupt and prejudiced against Caucasians (see Wright; Packer and Thomas; and Stannard, *Honor Killing*). Just two decades later, however, Wayne assures the audience that the Honolulu Police Department "rates A1 on an FBI list of municipal police departments." This image is reinforced by actor Dan Liu's competent and assured performance as the Chief of Police who, at the end of the movie, rescues Wayne from a beating and probably death at the hands of a communist gang.

As for the native population of Hawaii, gone are earlier images of bare-breasted warriors as in *South of Pago Pago*, topless hula-dancers like Delores Del Rio in *Bird of Paradise*, or the more modest but still sexy Clara Bow, with her naval showing, in *Hula*. Instead, we have native men in Aloha shirts, long pants, or a suit and tie, and female hula dancers dressed conservatively with their midriffs covered. All of the natives have a *hapa-haole* (half white) look, and there are no really dark-skinned actors on display. There are no interracial romances for the lead characters, and only one example of this in the whole film – a minor character *haole* married to a briefly glimpsed Japanese woman. Indeed, the color white dominates in this movie, whether it is the white of sailors' uniforms, the "whiter-than-white" motives of Wayne and Baxter, or the Caucasian actors who play virtually all of the lead character roles. For example, Madge (Veda Ann Borg), a loud *haole* woman, tells Wayne, "I wanna show you how we *kamaainas* live" as she takes him to both the Royal Hawaiian Hotel and a restaurant whose patrons are predominantly *haole* also. Madge's contention that she is a *kamaaina*, a "child of the land," reverses the role of native and interloper and is a common appropriation of both Hawaiian culture and political rights.

Even the Japanese are recruited into this reversal: while many suspects in the "sneak attack" murder of Baxter are Japanese, it is clear in the movie that the Japanese community has already been recruited as an American ally in the Cold War. Engelhardt states, "With remarkable speed in the immediate postwar years, three enemy nations, Germany, Japan, and Italy, became 'Free World' allies," more like "us" and less like "them" (58). For example, when a communist complains that Wayne attacked him without provocation, Police Chief Dan Liu states, "We all have provocation to attack you, [we're] all Americans." Similarly, the Japanese wife of communist spy Willie Namaka is portrayed sympathetically and now works as a nurse on a leper colony to atone for her earlier communist leanings. Like the old Japanese priest at a Shinto temple, Mrs. Namaka volunteers information willingly, as in the film's narrative all loyal "Americans" should. Just eight years earlier in *December 7*, John Ford was using these very same images to suggest the foreign, un-American nature of the Japanese in Hawaii. In a final bizarre twist, a Polish immigrant who has immigrated to the islands tells Wayne, "I came *here* to the West Coast," thus moving Hawaii thousands of miles east and closer to America.

Director Fred Zinnemann's *From Here To Eternity* leaves out the racial issues present both in James Jones's novel and in the military itself. For example, in the novel, Prew says to Violet, "Why in hell would I marry you? Have a raft of snot-nosed nigger brats? Be a goddam squawman and work in the goddam pineapple fields for the rest of my life? Or drive a Schofield taxi? Why the hell do you think I got in the Army? Because I didn't want to sweat my heart and pride out in a goddam coalmine all my life and have a raft of snot-nosed brats who look like niggers in the coaldirt" (112). Prew's reluctance to marry a non-Caucasian was also fueled by examples of disastrous interracial match-ups. For example, Jones describes Prew's views on "Dhom, the G Company duty sergeant, bald and massive and harassed, crossed his eyes, trailed by his fat sloppy Filipino wife and seven half-caste brats; no wonder Dhom was a bully, condemned to spend his life in foreign service like an exile because he had a Filipino wife" (111). These scenes and viewpoints are entirely omitted from the movie, as are virtually all references to race and racism in the military or in Hawaii. The *Variety* review states, "The bawdy vulgarity and the outhouse vocabulary, the pros and non-pros among its easy ladies, and the slambang indictment of Army brass have not been emasculated in the transfer to the screen, but are certainly shown in much better taste for consumption by a broader audience." *The New York Times* review also praises the movie's "job of editing, emending, re-arranging and purifying a volume bristling with brutality and obscenities" (2715).

These racial and sexual omissions make *From Here To Eternity* distinct from earlier movies that focus on these very themes to attract viewers. The movie hides racial difference and smoothes over Honolulu's sex industry and the military's role in it. The Hawaiian sex trade, that so attracted early moviemakers and, in World War II, was officially sanctioned by the U.S. military, marked Hawaii as different. To sailors, soldiers, airmen, and tourists, Hawaii represented a place other than America, a place where sex was readily available and interracial sex possible. As *From Here To Eternity* sanitizes or omits these facts altogether, it makes Hawaii less out of the ordinary and unusual, and instead transforms it into just another American community with everyday American problems.

From Here to Eternity has been praised for how successfully it evokes the sense of Hawaii in pre-war days. Such praise is deserved to the extent that the military scenes ring true. However, despite references to Kaneohe, the Kalakaua Inn, the Royal Hawaiian Hotel, and Kuhio Beach Park, and apart from the occasional Hawaiian or Chinaman appearing as a waitress or passerby, it is difficult to tell whether this is Hawaii or California. There is the occasional glimpse of Hawaii, such as a Hawaiian band playing in a restaurant, but even with the film's music the predominant song played throughout is "Re-enlistment Blues," sung by a Caucasian soldier. Neither does this movie feature the exotic scenery of earlier movies. Most of the action takes place inside Schofield Barracks or in Honolulu. Only one scene – Lancaster and Kerr's memorable romp at Kuhio Beach Park – reminds viewers of the exotic. This particular scene cannot, however, deflect attention away from the rest of the *mise en scène*, which is anything but exotic or, indeed, any different from a movie that could have been staged on any military base on the mainland United States.

The year 1955 seems to be a turning point in the South Seas film genre. Combined, of course, with other media, political policies and social factors – not the least of which was a political push for statehood – fourteen years of Hollywood movies emphasizing Hawaii as American seemed to have had the desired effect. With the "war story" embedded in the American consciousness, perhaps now the image of a thoroughly American Hawaii might be used in a different way. The year 1954 saw the momentous Supreme Court Case *Brown v. The Board of Education of Topeka*. Its outcome threatened to undermine America's whole social structure. Perhaps then Hawaii could be utilized as a successful example of the melting pot, of different races living together in harmony. From 1955 onwards, many Hollywood movies about Hawaii deal with issues of interracial relationships and racial intolerance albeit, for the most part, in a deliberately frothy and lightweight way. This reverses a recognized Cold War trend in Hollywood movie making of relegating social issues to the sidelines. As author Dennis McNally notes, "Raging anti-Communism clawed at American culture and disemboweled, among other things, American films; nearly one third of them had dealt with serious social themes in 1947, but in 1952 it was one eleventh" (108).

Many films in the "South Seas" genre reverse this Hollywood trend of demoting social issues. For example, *South Pacific* (1958) features an interracial relationship between a young American officer and a native girl. *Blue Hawaii* (1961) has *haole* Chad Gates (Elvis Presley) marrying a half-Hawaiian, half-French girl named Maile Duvall. *Diamond Head* (1963) features an oppressive American rancher named Richard Howland (Charlton Heston), who tries to stop his sister Sloan (Yvette Mimieux) from marrying Native Hawaiian Paul Kahana (James Darren). At the same time, as film critics Luis Reyes and Ed Rampell point out, Howland is "blind to hypocrisy and disclaiming racial discrimination" as he "carries on a clandestine love affair with the lovely Chinese Mei-Chen, who is to bear his son" (128). *Midway* (1976) features a sub-plot about race and prejudice concerning an American pilot and his Japanese-American fiancée. Of course, interracial relationships feature also in pre-World War II movies about Hawaii, but there is a different dynamic at work. Rarely do relationships between dark-skinned men and white women occur in these movies, such was the racial climate of the time. Houston Wood identifies only one movie, *White Heat* (1934), in which a Caucasian woman is attracted to a native man.

In these Hollywood movies, Hawaii acted as a role model for the turbulent mainland society of the late 1950s and onwards. Racial strife and civil unrest can be overcome, these movies suggest, if Hawaii acts as a paradigm for the way Americans handle racial issues. Nonetheless, the enduring image of Hawaii and other South Sea islands as a welcoming romantic paradise with sexually available natives still remained. In *Ma and Pa Kettle in Waikiki* (1955), for example, one character states, "Hawaii Waikiki, palms swaying in the moonlight. Oh it's just too romantic and wonderful." If it was an overstatement that "everybody wants to go to Hawaii," as actor James Darren states in *Gidget Goes Hawaiian* (1961), Hollywood movies were certainly ensuring, with their images both of half-dressed natives and under-dressed Americans, that Hawaii was the place to be for those Americans interested in forbidden or illicit interracial sex.

In the late 1950s and 1960s, the image of Hawaii as warm, feminized, and welcoming, and of its native people as sexually available, served as background for the type of interracial romances that had disappeared from this genre of movies decades before. In the early era of cinema, many films about Hawaii or the South Seas featured interracial romances. As Houston Wood notes, many of these movies include female Hawaiians of Royal ancestry who fall in love with the flotsam and jetsam of Westerners who wash up on Hawaii's shores: "The films suggest that Hawaiian women of such esteemed blood are worthy of the average American Davids and Keiths who pursue them. The dangers inherent in racial mixing are at the heart of these films, but they include acknowledgement of the possibility that these dangers can be surmounted if the Native is royal" (113). Wood observes that by the 1930s "racial mixing had become unequivocally unacceptable. When the racially tolerant *Aloha Oe* was remade as *Aloha* in 1931, the notion of a successful racial intermarriage was no longer offered in the final reel" (113).

This trend was reinforced by the Pearl Harbor attack, as it seemed that proof now existed that those deemed "foreign" (the Japanese), or "different" (brown-skinned Hawaiians), were as dangerous and devious as we had always been led to believe. In the movies, the disappearance of interracial romance continued throughout the 1940s and into the mid-1950s. However, as the *Brown* Supreme Court judgment gradually influenced changes in American society in the late 1950s and more extensively in the 1960s, the theme of interracial romance again began to permeate Hollywood's South Seas movies. While Caucasian characters remain foregrounded in these movies, and familiar stereotypes remain in portrayals of non-whites, the dramas and melodramas of interracial relationships began to reappear.

In *Enchanted Island* (1958), a film based loosely on Herman Melville's novel *Typee*, an American seaman has a passionate relationship with a beautiful native girl called Fayaway (Jane Powell). The sailors begin to suspect that the Typee are cannibals. When Tom disappears, and natives are seen wearing items of his clothing, Bedford turns away from Fayaway in disgust, believing her to have covered up Tom's grisly death.

However, he overcomes these feelings, realizing that he should not judge the Typee's customs, even if they appear abhorrent. Eventually, however, Fayaway and Bedford flee the Typee. Fayaway pays the price for her interracial romance when she is speared by the tribe's medicine man. Bedford, however, returns to the ship from which he fled and is, for some unexplained reason, promoted to first officer.

The novelty of interracial romance in *Enchanted Island* is lessened somewhat by this genre's traditional custom of employing a non-native actress in the role of a native. As in earlier movies, the audience is more accepting of miscegenation if the native does not display the physical characteristics of the supposedly inferior race. Nevertheless, unlike most movies about Hawaii or the South Seas made between 1941 and the mid-1950s, an interracial romance does at least occur. It may well be that in the racially aware atmosphere of the post-*Brown* era, Warner Brothers chose for that reason to release a movie based on a book that is considered to be sympathetic to natives and non-judgmental about interracial romance.

In *Mutiny on the Bounty* (1962), a Tahitian native girl called Maimiti (actress Taritatumi Teriipaia) falls in love with a British Naval officer, Fletcher Christian (Marlon Brando). That Maimiti is played by a real-life Polynesian woman is a significant change in direction for Hollywood. Luis Reyes states, "The producers felt from the start that a pure Polynesian should be selected to portray Maimiti" (Reyes and Rampell 214). In countless previous movies, native girls that have sexual or romantic relationships with Western men are played by non-native substitutes. Sometimes these actresses are obviously Caucasian, such as Dorothy Lamour in *Aloma of the South Seas* (1941), and sometimes they have the *hapa-haole* look and are played by Central or South American actresses such as Raquel Torres in *White Shadows in the South Seas* and Rita Moreno in *Pagan Love Song* (1950). It is perhaps because of the changing racial climate of the United States in the late 1950s and early 1960s that *Mutiny on the Bounty*'s promoters made such efforts to cast a genuine, dark-skinned native to play the role of an indigenous person.

That *Enchanted Island* and *Mutiny on the Bounty* are set in the historical past is perhaps a sign that Hollywood was still, however, treading carefully in the area of interracial romance. These movies did not cause race riots, or upset the social order, a fact that seems to have emboldened filmmakers. Most movies from this point on feature contemporary Hawaii, instead of historical Hawaii, and persist with the theme of interracial relationships. For example, *Gidget Goes Hawaiian* is a contemporary movie and an advertisement for Hawaii's tourist industry in 1961. While the movie is primarily about the romantic antics of a group of Caucasian American tourists, in one scene Gidget (Deborah Valley) surfs with a muscular, dark-skinned Native Hawaiian man. There is a sexual edge to their frolics: at one point, Gidget kneels on all fours at the front of a surfboard as the Hawaiian puts his head between her legs to lift her onto his shoulders. This scene is a carbon copy of the real-life frolics of some female Caucasian tourists with native beach boys in the 1930s. One Waikiki beachboy recalled a conversation with an American tourist in which she said, "When I was nineteen, you took me in tandem. Can you imagine what it was like for me, going to a Catholic school on the mainland, to have a man take me surfing? To sit on top of me, on the back of my legs. The thrill I had. Skin to skin" (qtd. in Desmond 126.). That night, Gidget's boyfriend Moondoggie (James Darren) sings a song that seems to be an ode to interracial romance:

> You hear the native boys all sighing, down on Mauna Loa Bay
> Cause when the Gidget goes Hawaiian, she goes Hawaiian all the
> way.
> Now there's a rumor on the island, she flirts with every passer-by,
> Cause when the Gidget goes Hawaiian, she catches each
> Hawaiian's eye.

A trio of Elvis Presley movies – *Blue Hawaii, Girls, Girls, Girls!* (1962) and *Paradise Hawaiian Style* (1966) – is also set in contemporary Hawaii. *Blue Hawaii* features Presley as *haole* Chad Gates. Like the character White Almond Flower in *The Idol Dancer* who had "the blood of vivacious France, inscrutable Java and languorous Samoa" running through her veins, Presley's girlfriend Maile Duvall (Joan Blackman) is half-Hawaiian and half-French. However, when she states, "My French blood tells me to argue with you and my Hawaiian blood tells me not to. They're really battling it out inside me," she is reversing the stereotype of early movies in the genre. For example, in *The Idol Dancer* it is White Almond Flower's French blood that makes her "civilized" and keeps her base "native" desires under control. In *Blue Hawaii*, however, Duvall's French side is problematic, while her Hawaiian blood supposedly gives her the welcoming, friendly characteristics that make her a personification of a contemporary, tourist-friendly Hawaii.

Floyd Matson notes that *Blue Hawaii* "trotted out nearly every confused stereotype of 'island' life and culture that had accumulated through the career of the South Sea syndrome" (40). However, the movie's racial themes are worthy of note: the interracial romance in *Blue Hawaii* was an early "first step" for Hollywood in the 1960s, a step that would lead eventually to the first interracial kiss between a European-American and an African-American on American television, between Captain James Kirk (William Shatner) and Uhura (Nichelle Nichols) in a 1968 episode of *Star Trek* entitled "Plato's Stepchildren."

Midway (1976) is an account of the 1942 battle that turned the tide of the war in the Pacific in America's favor. The movie mixes actual war footage with staged battles and also "borrows" scenes from another war movie entitled *Tora! Tora! Tora! Midway* is male-dominated and action-driven. Some of the most well known male actors of the "Greatest Generation" star, including Charlton Heston, Henry Fonda, Glenn Ford, James Coburn, and Robert Mitchum. To balance this over-abundance of testosterone, a subplot has Heston's son Ensign Tom Garth (Edward Albert) engaged to a Japanese-American girl called Haruko Sakura (Christina Kokubo). To add to the melodrama, Kokubo is a suspected spy and her parents are soon to be shipped to an internment camp on the United States mainland. Heston wrestles with his conscience about whether to help his possible future daughter-in-law. Eventually, he decides to call in favors with military intelligence and she is released.

Although the *Variety* review calls this a "phony subplot," this is more than a simple plot diversion. The context of this movie, made twenty-five years after the Pearl Harbor attack, was both ongoing Cold War animosities and a triumphant reminder of the values of America in the post-Vietnam War era. Like its predecessor *Tora! Tora! Tora!*, *Midway* allots significant portions of the movie to show the Japanese side of the battle. Neither do these movies feature racially demeaning stereotypes of the Japanese, as had many previous Pacific war movies. This is laudable, of course. However, both of these movies focus only on battle, and neglect to provide any social, political, or historical context. There is no discussion in either movie of, for example, the prelude to war or of the subsequent American response that ended at Hiroshima and Nagasaki. In fact, *Midway* reminds its audience that the atomic bombings were justified and that Hiroshima was a legitimate military target. On three separate occasions, for instance, the film connects the Japanese military to Hiroshima by use of subtitles. Not only is it where Admiral Yamamoto resides, the movie narrates, the Japanese Navy also leaves from Hiroshima Bay to attack Midway Island.

By focusing only on displays of military hardware, battle, and heroism, these movies tell a depoliticized, deracialized version of the war. For example, when a Japanese Admiral empathizes with a destroyed squadron of American planes and their "fourteen brave crews" who died like "our Samurai," the very real racial hatred felt by both sides in the conflict is erased from history. In fact, no one hates anyone in this movie, and war is portrayed as a passionless exercise conducted by masculine men just "doing their jobs." This movie is, therefore, very much a product of its time. In the post-World War II years, Japan was an ally of the United States: cinematic reminders of Japanese military barbarity would have been an unwelcome distraction from the Manichean Cold War narratives of good/bad, communist/democratic, red/red, white and blue that the U.S. government encouraged in the cinema and media. In these films, it was now acceptable to show the Japanese military as professional and brave. Professor David Desser notes,

> It was not until after the war that the United States could undertake a reconsideration of its opponents. Thus we find, years later, films that attempt to separate the Wehrmacht officer from his Nazi superiors, with such figures as Erwin Rommel emerging as ambiguously tragic heroes. And although it is significant in terms of how racism found its way into the Vietnam era, and into Vietnam War films, that we find more portrayals, more personifications, of our European former antagonists than our Asian enemies, we can still point to such films as *Hell in the Pacific* (1968), *Tora! Tora! Tora!* (1970), *Midway* (1976), and even the more recent *Farewell to the King* (1989) as endowing some human subjectivity to the Asian objects of America's aggression and blood-lust. (87)

The interracial love affair in *Midway* needs to be seen in the context of the Cold War zeitgeist. Americans and the Japanese were allied against the Soviet Union, and *Midway* therefore whitewashes and sanitizes issues such as the internment of over a thousand Japanese-Americans in Hawaii. Indeed, the internment camp in the movie looks more like a community center than a prison, and Kokubo's parents are docile and respectful towards Americans. Kokubo has the only raised voice of resistance and anger. She states, "Damn it, I'm an American! What makes us different from Italian-Americans or German-Americans?" One answer is, of course, racism. However, Heston replies, "Pearl Harbor, I suppose," thus excusing Americans from blame for internment by making it seem a "natural" reaction. *Midway*'s American audience had been preconditioned to accept such a sleight-of-hand by years of exposure to "sneak attack" narratives about Pearl Harbor.

In the post-Vietnam era, the theme of reconciliation – healing a divided nation – was prevalent in all aspects of American life.[4] The interracial relationship in *Midway* also serves as a healing act. While America waged war on an Asian people in Vietnam, *Midway* reminds its audience of the compassionate nature of Americans. For instance, Heston calls in favors and puts his career on the line to free Kokubo. The internment of Japanese is portrayed as, at worst, an understandable precaution, and compassionate Americans in authority like Heston allow the love affair between Kokubo and Albert to blossom, thus healing the wounds caused by war.

Assigning motives to a broad range of films released over a number of decades is a risky and imprecise venture. Noting that much of the Hawaii and "South Seas" genre fits neatly into Engelhardt's "war story" does not imply a structured plan or design by filmmakers. Instead, these themes illustrate how Hawaii has been imagined throughout the years and how it has been reshaped to fit the requirements of the American public. Sometimes, however, filmmakers misjudge those requirements. For example, it could be argued that the "lesson" Hawaii movies offered in interracial harmony in the late 1950s and 1960s went generally unheeded by Americans. Movie images of a racial paradise may have caused many Caucasian Americans to visit Hawaii to *escape* from racial tension on the mainland. Hawaii became the personification of an idealized, Arcadian America, sufficiently different from the mainland so that Americans could leave behind their everyday worries, but also sufficiently "American" as to be familiar and non-threatening. Desmond notes, for example, Hawaii gave American tourists a "sense of escape from domestic U.S. tensions [and] a feeling of still being in the United States (English predominates, no passport required for U.S. citizens, U.S. currency, U.S. brand names in hotels and products, etc.), and Hawaii provides a truly safe exoticism for white mainlanders. This experience reinforces their sense of still being the "core" of the American nation (Desmond 140).

Cinematic depictions of Hawaii, in war and peace, are less concerned with accuracy than they are with portraying Hawaii according to the needs of those on the U.S. mainland. According to these representations, until Western settlers arrived Hawaii used to be a desolate frontier inhabited by savages. It was their Manifest Destiny to "develop" a "virgin land" that was underutilized by its primitive, godless inhabitants. Westerners brought to Hawaii civilization, laws, technology, "progress," and Christianity. These settlers have written the story of Hawaii in a way that justifies their actions as beneficial and natural. In the twentieth century, the newly arrived medium of cinema reinforced these narratives. In the immediate aftermath of World War II, the idea of "American Hawaii" helped Americans cope with their guilt at the atomic bombings of Japan and deflected attention away from the racist nature of the Pacific war. In the late 1950s and 1960s, Hawaii acted as a paradigm for the mainland on interracial harmony. It is little wonder the thought of Native Hawaiian sovereignty is presently an anathema to the United States. For the U.S., Hawaii is the gift that keeps on giving.

Notes

1. In attempting to make sweeping statements about a large number of movies across a number of decades, it is perhaps useful to recall political scientist and media commentator Michael Parenti's disclaimer: "Do I select only the [movies and television shows] that paint the entertainment media in the worst possible light? If anything, I give disproportionately greater attention to the relatively few quality films and programs of progressive hue" (vii). In this study, I focus on those movies about Hawaii and the Pacific that are generally considered as the best examples of the genre such as *White Shadows of the South Seas* and *From Here To Eternity*. Parenti also reminds his critics, "For almost every criticism I make of the 'make-believe media,' one could find some exceptions" (vii).
Kahanamoku did appear in two post-war movies, *Wake of the Red Witch* (1948), and *Mister Roberts* (1955), neither of which are about Hawaii.
2. Of the 1946 strike, one labor union leader stated, "This victory makes Hawaii part of the United States for all Hawaiians, especially the workers. It is no longer a feudal colony" (Kent 135).
3. For example, Americans elected President Jimmy Carter, a relatively unknown Washington outsider, untainted by the Vietnam War or political scandals, partly on his promise to heal America's wounds. Movies also reflected this sense of healing: the main characters in *The Deer Hunter* (1978) sing, for example, a unifying, patriotic anthem, "God Bless America," in the film's climactic scene.

48

4. Film critic Gilbert Adair states, "[Director Michael] Cimino's intentions were... to restore his audience's confidence in their country's regenerative powers" (Adair 90).

Works Cited

Adair, Gilbert. *Hollywood's Vietnam*. London: William Heinemann, 1989.
Air Force. Dir. Howard Hawks. Warner Brothers, 1943.
Aloha Oe. Dir. Richard Stanton and Charles Swickard. Kay-Bee, 1915.
Albertini, Jim, Nelson Foster, Wally Inglis, amd Gil Roeder. *The Dark Side of Paradise: Hawaii in a Nuclear World*. Honolulu: Catholic Action of Hawaii/Peace Education Project, 1980.
Aloma of the South Seas. Dir. Alfred Santell. Paramount, 1941.
Bailey, Beth and David Farber. *The First Strange Place: Race and Sex in World War II Hawaii*. Baltimore and London: The Johns Hopkins UP, 1992.
Big Jim McLain. Dir. Edward Ludwig. Warner Brothers, 1952.
Bird of Paradise. Dir. King Vidor. RKO, 1932.
Bird of Paradise. Dir. Delmer Daves. Twentieth Century Fox, 1951.
Blue Hawaii. Dir. Norman Taurog. Hal Wallis Productions, 1961.
Brennan, Joseph L. *Duke: The Life Story of Hawai'i 's Duke Kahanamoku*. Honolulu: Ku Pa`a Publishing, 1994.
Brown, DeSoto. "Ebb Tide." *Honolulu Weekly* 10-16 Oct. 2001: 6-8.
Cook, James. *A Voyage to the Pacific Ocean. Undertaken, by the Command of His Majesty.* W. and A. Strahan, 1784.
December 7. Dir. John Ford. U.S. Navy, 1943.
The Deer Hunter. Dir. Michael Cimino. Universal, 1978.
Desmond, Jane. *Staging Tourism: Bodies on Display From Waikiki to Sea World*. Chicago: U of Chicago P, 1999.
Desser, David. "Charlie Don't Surf: Race and Culture in the Vietnam War Films." *Inventing Vietnam: The War in Film and Television*. Ed. Michael Anderegg. Philadelphia: Temple UP, 1991: 81-102.
Diamond Head. Dir. Guy Green. Columbia, 1963.
Dower, John. *War Without Mercy: Race and Power in the Pacific War*. New York: Pantheon, 1993.
Editors of the Army Times Publishing Company. *Pearl Harbor and Hawaii: A Military History*. New York: Bonanza, 1971.
Ellis, William. *Polynesian Researches during a residence of nearly six years in the South Sea Islands*. London, 1830.
Enchanted Island. Dir. Alan Dwan. Warner Brothers, 1958.
Engelhardt, Tom. *The End of Victory Culture: Cold War America and the Disillusioning of a Generation*. 2nd ed. U of Massachusetts P, 1998.
A Fallen Idol. Dir. Kenean Buel. Fox Film Corporation, 1919.

Ferguson, Kathy E. & Phyllis Turnbull. *Oh, Say, Can You See? The Semiotics of the Military in Hawaii.* Borderlines 10. Minneapolis: U of Minnesota P, 1999.

The Final Countdown. Dir. Don Taylor. Bryna Productions, 1980.

Flirtation Walk. Dir. Frank Borzage. Warner Brothers, 1934.

From Here to Eternity. Dir. Fred Zinnemann. Columbia Pictures, 1953.

Fussell, Paul. *Wartime: Understanding and Behavior in the Second World War.* New York: Oxford UP, 1990.

Gidget Goes Hawaiian. Dir. Paul Wendkos. Columbia, 1961.

Girls, Girls, Girls! Dir. Norman Taurog. Hal Wallis Productions, 1962.

Hawaii Calls. Dir. Edward F. Cline. RKO, 1938.

Honolulu. Dir. Edward Buzzell. MGM, 1939.

Hula. Dir. Victor Fleming. Paramount, 1927.

The Idol Dancer. Dir. D.W. Griffith. First National, 1920.

Jones, James. *From Here to Eternity.* 1951. New York: Dell, 1991.

Jungle Heat. Dir. Howard W. Koch. Bel-Air Productions, 1957.

Kent, Noel J. *Hawaii: Islands Under the Influence.* New York: Monthly Review Press, 1983.

Little Big Man. Dir. Arthur Penn. Cinema Center Films, 1970.

Ma and Pa Kettle in Waikiki. Dir. Lee Sholem. Universal International Pictures, 1955.

Matson, Floyd. "Hollywood Goes Hawaiian." *Viewers' Guide: East-West International Film Festival,* 40-41. Honolulu: East-West Film Festival, 1984.

McNally, Dennis. *Desolate Angel: Jack Kerouac, the Beat Generation, and America.* New York: Random House, 1980.

Melville, Herman. *Narrative of a Four Months' Residence among the Natives of a Valley of the Marquesas Islands.* London: John Murray, 1846.

Midway. Dir. Jack Smight. Universal, 1976.

Mutiny on the Bounty. Dir. Lewis Milestone. MGM, 1962.

Nanook of the North. Dir. Robert J. Flaherty. Les Frères Revillon, 1922.

The New York Times Film Reviews. Rev. of *From Here to Eternity* 6 Aug. 1953. New York: The New York Times and Arno Press, 1970: 2715.

---. Rev. of *Honolulu* 23 Feb. 1939. New York: The New York Times and Arno Press, 1970: 1580-1581.

---. Rev. of *Submarine Raider* 22 June 1942. New York: The New York Times and Arno Press, 1970: 1874.

Obeyesekere, Gananath. *The Apotheosis of Captain Cook: European Mythmaking in the Pacific.* Princeton and Honolulu: Princeton UP and Bishop Museum Press, 1992.

Packer, Peter and Bob Thomas. *The Massie Case.* New York: Bantam, 1966.

Pagan Love Song. Dir. Robert Alton. MGM, 1950.

Paradise Hawaiian Style. Dir. Michael D. Moore. Paramount Pictures, 1966.

Parenti, Michael. *Make-Believe Media: The Politics of Entertainment.* New York: St. Martin's Press, 1992.

Pearl Harbor. Dir. Michael Bay. Touchstone, 2001.

The Revolt of Mamie Stover. Dir. Raoul Walsh. Twentieth Century Fox, 1956.

Reyes, Luis and Ed Rampell. *Made in Paradise: Hollywood's Films of Hawaii and the South Seas.* Honolulu: Mutual, 1995.

Schmitt, Robert C. *Hawaii Data Book: A Statistical Reference to Hawaii's Social, Economic and Political Trends.* Honolulu: Mutual, 2002.

---. *Hawaii in the Movies 1898-1959.* Honolulu: Hawaiian Historical Society, 1988.

Sobchack, Thomas and Vivian Sobchack. *An Introduction to Film.* Boston: Little Brown & Co., 1980.

Soldier Blue. Dir. Ralph Nelson. AVCO Embassy Pictures, 1970.

South of Pago Pago. Dir. Alfred E. Green. Edward Small Productions, 1940.

South Pacific. Dir. Joshua Logan. Magna Corporation, 1958.

Stacpoole, Henry De Vere. *The Blue Lagoon.* Philadelphia: JB Lippincott, 1908.

Stannard, David E. *Before the Horror: the Population of Hawaii on the Eve of Western Contact.* Honolulu: U of Hawaii P, 1989.

---. *Honor Killing: How the Infamous "Massie Affair" Transformed Hawaii.* New York: Viking, 2005.

Stevenson, Robert Louis. *In the South Seas.* New York: Scribners, 1896.

Stewart, Charles. *A Visit to the South Seas in the U.S. Ship Vincennes, During the Years 1829 and 1830.* New York, 1831.

Submarine Raider. Dir. Lew Landers. Columbia, 1942.

Task Force. Dir. Delmer Daves. Warner Brothers, 1949.

Tin Pan Alley. Dir. Walter Lang. Twentieth Century Fox, 1940.

Tora! Tora! Tora! Dir. Richard Fleischer. Twnetieth Century Fox, 1970.

Trask, Haunani-Kay. *From a Native Daughter: Colonialism and Sovereignty in Hawaii.* Honolulu: U of Hawaii P, 1999.

---. "Settlers of Color and 'Immigrant' Hegemony: 'Locals' in Hawaii." *Amerasia Journal* 2 (2000): 1-24.

Twain, Mark "The Sandwich Islands." *New York Tribune* 6 Jan. 1873.

Variety Film Reviews. Rev. of *From Here to Eternity* 29 July 1953. New York and London: Garland, 1983.

---. Rev. of *Honolulu* 1 Feb. 1939. New York and London: Garland, 1983.

---. Rev. of *Midway* 16 June 1976. New York and London: Garland, 1983.

Waikiki Wedding. Dir. Frank Tuttle. Paramount, 1937.

White Heat. Dir. Lois Weber. Pinnacle Productions, 1934.

Wills, Gary. *John Wayne's America: The Politics of Celebrity.* Advance Uncorrected Reader's Proof. New York: Simon & Schuster, 1997.

Wood, Houston. *Displacing Natives: The Rhetorical Production of Hawaii.* Lanham, MD: Rowman & Littlefield, 1999.

Wright, Theon. *Rape in Paradise.* Honolulu: Mutual, 1990.

3

John Wayne and the Queer Frontier: Deconstructions of the Classic Cowboy Narrative during the Vietnam War

Christopher Le Coney and Zoe Trodd

"John Wayne?! You're gonna tell me that John Wayne's a fag?!"
—Midnight Cowboy (1969)

"I gave my dead d--- for John Wayne."
—Ron Kovic (1976)

"There ain't no queer in cowboy and I don't care for anyone suggesting there is," snapped Wyoming cowboy Jim-Bob Zimmerschied in December 2005 (qtd. in Sherwell). The growing numbers of participants at regional and national gay rodeo finals, and the existence of the International Gay Rodeo Association (founded in 1981 and now with member associations across most states, the District of Columbia, and two Canadian provinces) might suggest otherwise. But, responding to questions about Ang Lee's critically acclaimed film *Brokeback Mountain*, Zimmerschied continued: "I've been doing this job all my life and I ain't never met no gay cowboy...John Wayne and Will Rogers, they made real cowboy movies. They portrayed us like we are" (qtd. in Sherwell).

Nearly thirty years after his death, Wayne's name has been continually invoked in interviews, reviews, and articles sparked by the release of *Brokeback Mountain*. Ubiquitous in Western genre films from the 1930s through the 1970s, and a cultural icon of titanic proportions, Wayne's tall stature, chiseled jaw, and broad shoulders made him the perfect celluloid cowboy. His performances set the standard by which all

Hollywood cowboys – including Ang Lee's – were then judged. "I think my career demonstrates that I am no panty-waist," Wayne told a *Playboy* journalist in 1971 (Wayne 92), and this decades-long career had made Wayne a poster-boy for strong, independent, American masculinity. Wayne's was also a heterosexual masculinity. His on and off screen personas were unambiguously straight: on screen he idealized a vision of virile straight men who waged battle by day and wooed women by night, and off-screen his personal demeanor and political values seemingly mirrored those of his cowboy characters. He espoused conservative causes, repeatedly expressed a personal distaste for homosexuality, particularly its pervasive presence in Hollywood, and proclaimed himself disgusted by Tennessee Williams' *Suddenly Last Summer* (1959). "They've gone and killed John Wayne with this movie," concluded Zimmerschied of *Brokeback Mountain* (qtd. in Sherwell). But while Lee's portrayal of gay cowhands in *Brokeback Mountain* might be an affront to the John Wayne myth of an exclusively heterosexual frontier, it is by no means the first. Since the late 1960s, this cultural myth has been under attack.

John Schlesinger's Western, Vietnam, and a Frontier Dystopia

It was a brisk January day in 1974 and the citizens of Cambridge did not know what to make of the spectacle. A boisterous crowd of nearly 400 Harvard students was milling about a military armored personnel-carrier as it made its way down Mt. Auburn Street towards the *Harvard Lampoon* office. All eyes were fixed upon the 6'4" barrel-chested figure who stood atop the tank with an unloaded gun, smiling and waving casually as he dodged the occasional incoming snowball. Cambridge's celebrity visitor was none other than John Wayne, celluloid cowboy extraordinaire and the recent recipient of the *Lampoon*'s Brass Balls Award, given in recognition of his "machismo" and his "penchant for hitting people in the mouth" (Kifner 41). An article in the *New York Times* noted that although Wayne was foraying into "hostile territory," he managed to charm the liberal-leaning campus community. The *Lampoon* had invited him to take part in a political debate in which he answered pointed questions on his conservative politics. A handful of Native American activists protested his appearance but, despite the obstacles, the Duke dominated the day's proceedings with his mix of rough bravado, folksy humor, and sincere disregard for the academy's liberal sensitivities. The *New York Times* even summed up the day's debate by painting Wayne as a modern-day

Theodore Roosevelt – a "symbol of American mythology: cowboy, soldier, agent of empire" (Kifner 41).

Wayne dominated Harvard that winter day, just as his character Dunson had dominated the body and spirit of Matthew Garth in Howard Hawks's *Red River* (1948). Ironically, however, *Red River* is one of several pre-Stonewall counter-westerns: *The Outlaw* (1943), *The Left-Handed Gun* (1958), and *Red River* are all charged with homo-eroticism. But while the gay sub-currents of these pre-Stonewall films occasionally bubble up in moments of release, any up-swellings are usually mitigated, subdued, or window-dressed. It was not until the 1969 release of both *Lonesome Cowboys* and *Midnight Cowboy* that homoerotic undercurrents within the western genre reached the point of overflow. Much ink has been spilled by critics debating whether Joe and Rizzo's relationship in *Midnight Cowboy* is homosexual, for it resists a conclusive label (though even Wayne could not ignore its explicit interrogation of cowboy sexuality: answering a *Playboy* interviewer's question about "perverted" films, Wayne responded, "Wouldn't you say that...*Midnight Cowboy*, a story about two fags, qualifies? But don't get me wrong; as far as a man and woman are concerned, I'm awfully happy there's a thing called sex" [76]). However, the true significance of John Schlesinger's 1969 film lies in this critical debate itself: *Midnight Cowboy* marks a tentative yet clear turning-point in the history of the Hollywood western.

Midnight Cowboy is the tale of a Texan named Joe Buck who takes a bus to New York in search of rich women who will hire him as a hustler, but who instead ends up spending a hard winter with a con artist named Ratso Rizzo. As Joe leaves Texas in the film's opening moments, he passes an abandoned movie theatre whose marquee still advertises the last film shown, Wayne's *The Alamo* (1960). That film has a special place in John Wayne's filmography, for Wayne not only starred but also directed and produced it as his personal pet project. The abandoned movie theater suggests a masculine icon in peril – another toppled, empty myth – and anticipates the situation in New York, where macho gay cowboy clones further undermine masculine signifiers. In fact, another toppling strategy employed by Schlesinger is to focus on the largely performative foundations of the macho cowboy myth. Joe wears a snappy, tight-fitting cowboy outfit complete with western boots and a hat, and the camera frequently dwells on booted feet walking or cowboy hats bouncing along the street, yet women wear faux western outfits, and gay male hustlers dress as cowboy clones. Schlesinger's clones emphasize the fragility of the macho cowboy myth, as Rizzo explains: "That great big dumb cowboy crap of yours don't appeal to nobody, except every Jackie on 42nd street! That's faggot stuff! You want to call it by its name, that's strictly for fags!" In reply, Joe stammers: "John Wayne?! You're gonna tell me that John Wayne's a fag?!" This tentative, yet open vocalization of the homoerotic subcurrents in westerns signaled a shift in the cultural landscape: fissures had formed in the cowboy's identity, in part because of the pervasive presence of frontier language and imagery during the Vietnam war.[1]

The resurgence of frontier rhetoric loomed large as early as 1960, when John F. Kennedy's Democratic Party Nomination acceptance speech observed: "From the lands that stretch 3000 miles behind me, the pioneers of old gave up their safety, their comfort and sometimes their lives to build a new world here in the West.... But the problems are not all solved and the battles are not all won, and we stand today on the edge of a new frontier." Seven years later American politicians and generals called hostile Vietnam "Indian country" and referenced "Daniel Boon Squads." In *Dispatches*, for example, Michael Herr claims that a captain invited him to play cowboys and Indians. Vietnam had become a movie: approached by politicians like a western and fought by cowboy-generals and soldiers with expectations of what veteran Ron Kovic later called "the glory John Wayne war" (158). The silver-screen myth of the West seemed to be informing America's ongoing struggle in Vietnam: a pioneer cavalry entered a wilderness of savages, and Kovic, for one, felt like "your John Wayne come home," as the first-edition cover to his Vietnam memoir put it.

Conflated in the American imagination were frontier myths, the Vietnam War, and the cult of John Wayne. As Richard Slotkin explains in *Gunfighter Nation*, the frontier myth "provided an imaginative model of the kind of historical actor who is needed in a struggle of this kind." The "new enemy does not fight by civilized rules," Slotkin continues, and so "can only be defeated by someone who combines the amoral pragmatism and technical expertise of the gunfighter with the skill in handling natives that belongs to the 'man who knows Indians'" (446). Slotkin adds that the "historical past was itself encoded in the terms of myth...the scenarios and game-models developed by the policy-makers were not very different from the imaginative projections that were developed by fiction writers and filmmakers.... Tropes and symbols derived from Western movies had become one of the more important interpretive grids through which

Americans tried to understand and control their unprecedented and dismaying experiences in Vietnam" (546). And, while history became a movie, movies about Vietnam referenced frontier-history. Directors, unwilling to make explicit antiwar movies, transformed Vietnam into the Indian frontier: *Soldier Blue* (1970) and *Little Big Man* (1970) drew parallels between the Sand Creek and Wichita River massacres of 1864 and 1868, and the My Lai massacre of 1968. Westerns made between 1965 and 1972 were often about Vietnam, and Vietnam continued to be represented as a western: after the war, *The Deer Hunter* (1978) revisited Vietnam as a mythic frontier, drawing upon James Fenimore Cooper's *The Deerslayer* (1841), and in *Full Metal Jacket* (1987) a soldier asks, "Is that you, John Wayne? Is this me?" while another comments, "I'll be General Custer, but who'll be the Indians?"

Only one Vietnam film was made while the war unfolded: *The Green Berets* (1968), a propagandist movie partly sponsored by the Department of Defense and the only feature film of the period to support American involvement in Vietnam. Wayne directed and starred as Colonel Kirby, named after a character in *Fort Apache* (1948). The Montagnard outpost becomes "Dodge City," and Wayne's western persona blends with his other significant genre role as a soldier. The film's producer even admitted: "when you're making a picture, the Indians are the bad guys" (qtd. in Suid 233). Thus helping to sustain America's cowboy dreams on the silver screen – offering the frontier cowboy as a model American soldier – Wayne also translated those dreams into *Realpolitik*, becoming a vocal supporter of the war.

Yet by 1968 the war had begun to undermine Americans' confidence in their classic cowboy and Indian narratives; cultural myths of an Anglo-American aggressor who always triumphed over the colored Other. "I gave my dead d--- for John Wayne and Howdy Doody," wrote Kovic (whose war-wounds left him impotent), also describing "a generation of violence and madness, of dead Indians and drunken cowboys" (98, 158). Doctors dubbed a post-Vietnam stress disorder the "John Wayne Syndrome," and Kovic's disillusionment with this war echoed across war journalism, veteran memoirs, and interviews. One Marine in *Dispatches* hates the movie he is in, and another veteran recalled: "When I went to Vietnam, I believed in Jesus Christ and John Wayne. After Vietnam, both went down the tubes. It don't mean nothin'" (qtd. in Mahedy 33). Still another recounted: "I lost my footing and slipped into a ditch, went under the water and came up and out, screaming, 'This ain't a war movie! This ain't a John Wayne movie!'.... It took me six months in Vietnam to wake up.... [Movies] could no longer help me to deflect reality" (qtd. in Bird 11). America was finding no regeneration through violence in Vietnam. In 1970, journalist Saul Pett observed: "We walk safely among the craters of the moon but not in the parks of New York or Chicago or Los Angeles. Technology and change run berserk, headlights hide by day and moral values shred overnight. The unthinkable multiplies until it seems 'things fall apart – the center cannot hold'.... America is no longer immune to history.... America, we seem suddenly to have discovered, is no longer infinite in space or resources or hope. There is no next valley or virgin forest to tread" (qtd. in Roberts and Olson 586). Echoing Frederick Jackson Turner's 1893 pronouncement of the closing of the frontier, Pett's article re-declared the end of cowboy dreams: someone tell John Wayne the cowboy is not invincible.

Wayne was a standard-bearer for the American right, and he came under attack from Native American groups, feminists, and gay rights groups, as well as from anti-war protesters. After all, when inviting Wayne to Harvard, the *Lampoon* had written: "We've heard you're supposed to be some kind of legend, everybody talks about your he-man prowess... You think you're tough. We're not so tough. We dare you to have it out, head on, with young whelps here who call the supposedly unbeatable John Wayne, the biggest fraud in history" (qtd. in Kifner 41). Though Wayne often fought back against criticism, frequently offering incendiary comments to the press, the students' confrontational language and ironic cynicism were indicative of Wayne's contested legacy in the wake of campus anti-war sentiment.[2]

Activists from all of the 1960s major protest movements turned the pervasive frontier mythology back on those perpetuating it and appropriated the cowboy soundtrack to Vietnam. Within the context of the Native American protest movement, some activists argued that if history were repeating itself, then – contrary to Marx's famous dictum that it repeats first time as tragedy, second time as farce – Vietnam repeated a tragedy: "history repeats itself and this is not the first time that American soldiers have murdered women and children...how about Wounded Knee?", observed a letter to *Life* magazine in 1969 (qtd. in White 46). A protest image by Roland Winkler, published in the journal *Akwesasne Notes* in 1974, juxtaposed North American Indians with Vietnamese, connected by a flag in the shape of the Statue of Liberty superimposed, and Dee Brown's *Bury My Heart at Wounded Knee* (1970) sold over five million copies within two years: Brown's success was due in part to the situation in Vietnam, for his book's publication coincided with protests against the war that pointed to the inherent violence of American culture and sought previous examples of America's empire mentality. If there were connections between the wars at home and abroad, then protest over Vietnam could inspire and fuel protest over domestic abuses of power. American Indian Movement (AIM) members, many of whom were Vietnam veterans, identified with anti-Vietnam war protestors, connecting American imperialism abroad and at home. Activists drew comparisons between Vietnam and Wounded Knee, then returned to the site of Wounded Knee for a battle with U.S. armed forces and a 71-day occupation from March to May 1973 – one of AIM's most high-profile protests. "The best analogy is South Viet Nam," insisted Kenneth Tilson, an attorney fighting the government's illegal invasions of reservations. "Most obviously, there is a corrupt government of natives, who are set up, armed, supplied, financed, propagandized for, and maintained in power by the U.S. Government" (qtd. in *Voices* 128).

Some wondered if contemporary Indian wars were in fact preparation for Vietnam: "we used to talk about 'bringing the war home,'" said Bruce Elison recently. "[T]he FBI...thought that that was really a good idea, and many of the tactics that they used in Indochina and Central America and other places in this world, they decided to try out on the Pine Ridge Reservation" (n.p.). The U.S. government did "bring the war home": one government agency ran a public campaign linking the Black Panthers to the Vietcong. But, again, activists turned this connection around. Beyond AIM, the late 1960s and early 1970s saw Civil Rights and Black Power protesters make the connection between the wars at home and abroad. On January 6, 1966, the Student Non-Violent Coordinating Committee issued a public position paper that connected lynching to the Vietnam war: "The murder of Samuel Young in Tuskegee, Alabama, is no different than the murder of peasants in Vietnam," they said. "Samuel Young was murdered because the United States law is not being enforced. Vietnamese are murdered because the United States is pursuing an aggressive policy in violation of international law" (416). The Panthers were soldiers at war in "the jungle which is America," added Reginald Major (280), and in 1967 Huey Newton set Vietnam in a history of racist policies: "The enslavement of black people from the very beginning of this country, the genocide practiced on the American Indians and the confining of the survivors on reservations, the savage lynching of thousands of black men and women…and now the cowardly massacre in Vietnam, all testify," he claimed, "to the fact that toward people of color the racist power structure of America has but one policy: repression, genocide, terror, and the big stick" (7). If the race war raged abroad, it also continued at home: "As the aggression of the racist American government escalates in Vietnam, the police agencies of America escalate the repression of black people throughout the ghettoes of America," said Newton (8). In 1969, a letter in *Life* magazine reiterated the connections between domestic racial upheaval and the Vietnam counterinsurgency: "We have thousands of Mylais every day right here in America," said the reader, "the brutalizing of individuals in the everyday life of urban communities…. We accept killing, the killing of civilians in Vietnam and the killing here in Chicago of the head of the black Panthers, as…a way of life" (qtd. in White 46).

Betty Friedan then connected the feminist movement and the Vietnam war; a war seemingly driven by America's frontier mythology and its well-established vision of ideal masculinity. She recalled seeing male anti-war protesters in 1968, "saying they didn't have to napalm all the children in Vietnam and Cambodia to prove they were men," and realizing that they were "defying the masculine mystique as we had defied the feminine mystique" (391-2). Connecting the feminist movement to the anti-war movement, she explained in 1973, "I believe the locked-up sexual energies have helped to fuel, more than anyone realizes, the terrible violence erupting in the nation and the world during the past ten years. If I am right, the sex-role revolution will liberate those energies from the service of death and will make it really possible for men and women to 'make love, not war'" (395). Adrienne Rich made a similar connection between masculinity and war in her 1976 sequence of lesbian-love sonnets, "Twenty-One Love Poems": "You know, I think that men love wars," she wrote. "And they still control the world, and you are not in my arms" (35).

Slotkin documents how the western genre was beset by "counterculture Westerns" in the early 1970s, and links this to Vietnam and race-based protest (631). In part, the 1960s marked the beginning of the end for the hegemonic legacy of Theodore Roosevelt's conception of the American West. While cowhands in the nineteenth century were a group of diverse races and ethnicities, Roosevelt white-washed demographic realities to portray them as distinctly white heroes of the frontier. But while Slotkin explores how race defined Roosevelt's conception of the frontier, he largely ignores the gender dynamics at work in that conception. Gail Bederman's *Manliness and Civilization* goes some way toward correcting this oversight, explaining that Roosevelt's racial philosophy was inextricably related to his schematic understanding of gender roles in civilized society (18), and, extending this observation to the 1960s, Martin Pumphrey singles out feminism to argue that protest movements asked modern audiences to view the western and Wayne's cowboy masculinity as anachronistic and ironic (93). Pumphrey's focus upon gender counterbalances Slotkin's focus upon race, but neither critic discusses sexuality in their examinations of counter-cultural challenges to the western – in spite of Schlesinger's "perverse" story "about two fags" and Andy Warhol's flamboyantly queer western of 1969, *Lonesome Cowboys*.

Yet gay rights activists also questioned the acceptance of an exclusively heterosexual American frontier, again confirming the domestic roots of America's mess abroad and undermining the cultural myths and stereotypes that America had enshrined in the form of Wayne's westerns. Some envisaged an exclusively homosexual utopia instead. Carl Wittman's "Refugees from Amerika" called for free, self-governed territory. L. Craig Schoonmaker, leader of Homosexuals Intransigent!, wanted to make gays a majority, suggesting migration to certain city neighborhoods and the takeover of election districts. He recommended beginning with Manhattan's 19th and 20th Congressional Districts and called this the first Gay Power district (qtd. in Teal 292). Don Jackson wanted to take over Alpine County, in California's Sierra Nevada, and turn it into a "Stonewall Nation." At a Berkeley gay liberation conference in December 1969, he laid out his gay nationalist vision: "A beautiful valley in the mountains...A place where a gay government can build the basis for a flourishing gay counter-culture and city...There is a county in California where 200 gays would constitute a majority of registered voters...The colony could become the gay symbol of liberty, a world center for the gay counter-culture, and a shining symbol of hope to all gay people in the world." Jackson asked pioneers to help form this Stonewall Nation (qtd. in Teal 292-4).

Amid these calls for a new, gay frontier space, gay cowboys began to peek further out of the proverbial closet. Clones appeared within the queer community in the late 1960s and early 1970s: gay men who adopted an overtly butch fashion style that looked to traditional images of masculinity for inspiration (the biker, the lumberjack, the construction worker, and of course, the cowboy). "It would be unlikely for an American boy growing up [in the 1960s] not to have a cowboy hero," explained one gay man to fashion historian Shaun Cole (127), and clones (so named because they all looked alike) were particularly drawn to the cowboy – in large part because cowboys were larger-than-life masculine icons. Then *Lonesome Cowboys* and reclaimed the silver screen frontier as a space for gay cowboys.

Midnight Cowboy's connection to Vietnam is most powerfully established during the nightmare sequence. When Joe is anally raped in a frantic dream with terrifying flashbacks, the John Wayne myth of heterosexual masculinity is sodomized right along with him. The dream sequence depicts a violent gang-bang. Joe's girlfriend Annie is ripped from his arms, leaving him to be raped by a male posse while she is assaulted in the distance. Joe wakes and yells: "Where my boots, where are my damn boots?!" His dream of rape becomes an almost-castration, felt in the absence of his cowboy boots. Even more significantly, the first thing he hears upon waking is the sound of a radio anchor announcing the latest death toll in Vietnam. He grabs the radio out of Rizzo's hands and switches it off, but cowboy identity, the Vietnam war, and the traumatic rape have collapsed into each other: the scene symbolizes the psychological rape of American warrior-masculinity suffered in Vietnam.[3]

The real-life frontier space of Texas – as well as the filmic frontier so long kept open by Wayne – has been closed. But *Midnight Cowboy* offers little by way of a new frontier space, for Schlesinger's vision of an alternative remains decidedly dystopian. Joe's decision to abandon his dead-end existence as a dishwasher in small-town Texas and depart for New York had seemingly constructed Manhattan as the new frontier space. In the shower before departing Texas, he sings: "Whoopee yi yo! Git along, little doggie, for you know New York will be your new home." The song is a classic Western tune, but the traditional lyrics, as first composed by Owen Wister in 1893, are: "you know that Wyoming will be your new home." The substitution of New York for the Cheyenne State inverts the traditional East to West frontier narrative, but New York turns out to be no modern utopia. Increasingly lost and dejected, Joe runs out of money and wanders the streets of Gotham that have become his own dystopic urban jungle. As though emphasizing this closing of the frontier, Joe's New York dream sequence includes numerous scenes in which shallow visual fields and jarring camera angles create a sense of claustrophobic entrapment. Several shots in the dream sequence show him trapped in the dead-end of a New York alley, or with his face pressed against a barbed-wire fence (like those that closed off the frontier and ended cattle drives in the great plains). Initially trapped in Texas, he now finds himself trapped in New York. For, if the 1960s saw a crisis in America's frontier mythology, then Joe is confronting a post-frontier reality: what Herr describes as "the turnaround point where [history] would touch and come back to form a containing perimeter" (49).

Rizzo, on the other hand, dreams of Florida, rather than New York. He adorns his derelict building with brightly-colored posters depicting sunny skies and bountiful orange groves. But his imagined Florida utopia is also a no-place. One of his daydreams begins with the pair running happily along a beach, but it quickly turns nightmarish. Then, toward the end of the film, shots of passing scenery seen through the bus window on the way to Miami, echo similar scenes from Joe's journey to New York. This framing device in the film echoes Herr's "containing perimeter" in its circularity. There's no frontier left and Rizzo and Joe run in vain, as a sign glimpsed earlier in the film had prophesied: at one point Joe's Manhattan-bound bus passed a roadside motel with a bright neon sign that reads, "The El Dorado." Just as that mythic land kept the Spaniards searching in vain, so the effort to find a new American frontier is similarly thwarted. Rizzo dies on the bus to Miami leaving Joe alone. Florida is still out of reach for Rizzo – and for Rizzo and Joe as a pair – and the film ends with Joe discarding his cowboy costume. Having woken from an actual dream to hear bad news about America's latest "Indian War" on the radio, Joe now hears the broader wake-up call for a country cowboy-dreaming its way through a war.

Andy Warhol's Western, the Gay Rights Movement, and a Queer Frontier

Throughout the 1960s, the growing visibility and activism of racial, feminist, and gay minority groups fermented social unrest and pushed Americans to re-examine long-held assumptions about what made men "men." The acceptance of heterosexual hegemony was being challenged on multiple fronts by gay rights groups, and, while *Midnight Cowboy* had connected the gay cowboy to the crisis in Vietnam, *Lonesome Cowboys* used the figure of the gay cowboy to connect the 1960s gay rights movement to earlier forms of gay activism. In particular, *Lonesome Cowboys* engages the gay rights movement's internal debate over the acceptance of effeminate "fairies." This issue had been a point of heated debate within the gay community for quite some time. As homophobic persecution increased during the Lavender Scare of the early Cold War period, new organizations were formed to address the needs of the gay community. The two most famous of these were The Mattachine Society, founded in 1951 by gay rights activist Harry Hay, and a more radical off-shoot organization called ONE, which aggressively agitated for gay rights in the 1950s. The differing politics of these organizations is clear from the debate surrounding effeminate or "fairy" gay men, which tapped into the deeper issue of how gays understood themselves through traditional gender paradigms. The Mattachine Society's more conservative tendencies and its aversion to the taint of Communism marginalized more flamboyant homosexuals, as evidenced in the topic of one meeting: "What can we do about those swishes and dykes that give us a bad name?" ONE took the opposite course, embracing a vision of a distinct gay minority identity and fashioning a broad-based, radical approach.

Activist Jim Kepner attended the Mattachine meeting that addressed the perceived problem of "swishes and dykes." He recounts that the discussion included repeated complaints that flamboyant gays were hindering the movement by making heterosexuals uncomfortable, until he finally protested – reminding the group that "it was those obvious ones who established squatter's rights to the Gay bars that the rest of us could sneak in and out of" (3). Continuing to insist that it was flamboyant gays, already marginalized by their obvious nature, who had initiated the homophile movement, Kepner went on to write an editorial for ONE magazine, in 1954, lambasting those gays who "puritanically attack swishes and fairies, insisting they'd never associate with such trash." Kepner's editorial explained: "They will try to excommunicate any homosexual who belies their view that we aren't really different. Neither rebels, nor swishes, nor any others who fall short of their standards of respectability will be welcome in their society.... Is our aim to pacify, or to fight?... I am interested in defending my right to be as different as I damn please. And I've picked up the notion that I can't protect my own rights without fighting for everyone else's" (16).

The debate between Mattachine and ONE over effeminate gays was soon rendered obsolete by the Stonewall riots: that night on Christopher Street marked the beginning of a fundamental shift in the politics of gay rights activism. But this short history of the homophile movement's differing attitudes towards effeminate gay men offers another perspective from which to view the subversion of the John Wayne cowboy image by *Lonesome Cowboys*, with its campy cowboys, and *Midnight Cowboy*, with its uber-masculine clones. In *Lonesome Cowboys*, there is no longer anything "unspoken" about the love that dare not speak its name: Warhol constructs a Wild Wilde West and a gay utopia that stands in stark contrast to the dystopia imagined by Schlesinger. Even more importantly, however, *Lonesome Cowboys* offers a frontier utopia where an effeminate cowboy might exist. The town sheriff is an occasional transvestite, and one character notes that they have always been accepting of him: "we always respect you…when you got your new wig, no one said anything – we even drove you into town." Warhol depicts a relationship of tolerance between the macho gay cowboy and the drag queen sheriff, a union of seeming opposites.

Throughout the film, Warhol's campy cowboys subvert the hyper-masculine John Wayne stereotype. The narrative begins as a curly-haired brunette named Ramona travels the Southwest with her male nurse. They wander the abandoned streets of an ordinary-looking frontier town in Arizona, "looking for a little companionship." The nurse is immediately coded as gay in traditional Hollywood fashion, with his high-pitched lisp and swishing gait. He soon comments of an empty church that "an altar boy would have done…for either of us." The pair is then greeted by a band of five "brothers" that ride into town, and a quarrel quickly develops. Ramona questions the brothers' sexuality, and her nurse makes sexual comments ("look at that man, with a bulge in his pants!"). Enraged, the eldest brother Louis yells, "Listen sheriff – tell these creeps – tell them that they can't walk around staring at my brothers…those people are perverts," but his siblings respond warmly with awkward smiles, bowing their heads coyly as the camera lingers on their faces and bodies.

The film shifts to an extended campground scene, where the mostly-naked "brothers" share sleeping bags and cavort in an extended homoerotic wrestling match. The nurse pairs up with one of the younger brothers, prompting Ramona to remark: "But you came out here to cure your perversion." The nurse is explicitly rejecting the nineteenth-century vision of the frontier as a site of male regeneration, while the wrestling match mocks the warrior-masculinity of those regenerated men. *Lonesome Cowboys* then moves towards a new vision of the frontier. One of the younger brothers yells at Louis for spending the night with a newcomer named Tom: "I was supposed to sleep with him last night!" Louis ignores his brother and tells Tom, "I want you to stay with us, be a part of us if you can...you're so beautiful." The film ends with the pairing of Louis and Tom, who ride off into the sunset, bound for California – a frontier space with "lots of beautiful men," as Louis promises, adding: "It's great, you can get anything you want out there." The space of the Western frontier wilderness is explicitly marked in opposition to the East: "How can you learn life if you're in the East where they have books, mathematicians, and reading?" one cowboy remarks. "You should be out here, under the trees of life." There is something "under the trees" that offers these cowboys their regenerative frontier: a utopia regenerated through desire rather than violence. *Lonesome Cowboys* even had the original title of *Ramona and Julian*: if camp is the opposite of tragedy, then these names are significant. Warhol inverts the genders of Shakespeare's *Romeo and Juliet*, and his parodic inversion suggests that *Lonesome Cowboys* rejects the tragic queer-frontier narrative; strains of which are evident in films like *The Outlaw, The Left-Handed Gun*, and *Red River*, which variously kill off the queer cowboy, allow him to remain but control latent subversiveness within the trappings of heterosexuality, or banish him to Mexico. Not abandoning but rather adapting America's cowboy dreams, Warhol offers a renewed vision of the West as what might be termed a homotopia. John Wayne would be skeptical, but Ang Lee's Jack Twist would surely approve.

To argue that Warhol is queering the frontier, and attacking the John Wayne myth of a heterosexual frontier world, is to run contrary to many critics. For example, Mark Finch, former co-programmer of the London Gay and Lesbian Film Festival, notes that "*Cowboys* doesn't lay any claims to being a political statement," and asserts "the absence of easy links between the film's form and this crucial moment in civil rights politics" (117). Finch misses the political and historical significance of *Lonesome Cowboys* because he insists that the film has little in common with traditional westerns. Yet the film's narrative is set at the turn of the twentieth century: the backdrop scenery depicts a classic frontier town with hastily erected wooden structures and dusty unpaved roads, and the characters dress in period attire while playing classic western roles (sheriff, outlaw-cowboys, and the lone woman lost in an otherwise exclusively male world). Staying true to the genre, Warhol's camp aesthetic was able to manipulate it, allowing the film to take aim at the self-important mythology that had infused westerns since the 1930s. Warhol even shot the film at the Old Tucson set in Arizona, where John Wayne had filmed on numerous occasions. Undermining Wayne's hyper-straight cowboy with its fake fellatio and naked all-male romping scenes, *Lonesome Cowboys* simultaneously soils the physical space of the Old Tucson set. Like Schlesinger, Warhol mocks the abandoned mausoleum of myth.

Another aspect of Warhol's strategy in toppling the mythology of Westerns is to imbue his film with overtones of a post-Western. Before the narrative proper is an extended soft-core sex scene between a curly-haired brunette (the as-yet unidentified Ramona) and her blond Adonis lover. This opening is incongruous with the rest of the film, but it sets the central theme of Warhol's western: sex. The scene is too mechanical to be erotic and too tedious to be pornographic; it takes the blond lover nearly four, drawn-out minutes to remove his pants. In fact, the scene is so oddly mundane that the viewer's attention gravitates towards the background rock music: "At the old Rialto theater, the West that lives on the screen brightens up the mezzanine. There I sit stretching wide, just like Lonesome Cowboys ride. At Rialto intermissions, when the dudes slip around...I let my mind turn away, and dream again about the day that I be Lonesome Cowboy bound." This soundtrack throws the already-confused viewer further off-balance by introducing a self-reflexivity ("the West that lives on the screen"). The film's opening strategy repeats throughout: Warhol continually seeks to highlight the discrepancy between the genre's supposed reality and the frontier's actual reality, often through jarring and self-reflexive juxtapositions between a scene's visual message and the soundtrack's spoken one. In addition, the track emphasizes the escapist, fantasy quality of the singer's identification with the Rialto's celluloid cowboys. Along with Warhol's abrupt opening, mechanical sex scene, and the meta-references throughout, it promises a wake-up call from old-school cowboy dreams.

Unlike Schlesinger, Warhol offered the potentially radical vision of a utopian queer frontier; an attractive alternative to America's fast-spoiling cowboy dreams. Still, the film's dependence on a camp aesthetic reinforces many of the pre-Stonewall stereotypes of effeminate queers, for though the brothers are not as flamboyant as the nurse, most of them "swish" to some extent. Revolutionary as his film was, Warhol's gay cowboys perhaps posed less of a threat to male masculinity than the butch Times Square clones of *Midnight Cowboy*. Yet the public reaction to these films indicates a greater degree of comfort with Schlesinger's film: *Midnight Cowboy*, a feature film release by a major Hollywood Studio (United Artists), was a huge success with critics and at the box-office, going on to win seven Academy Award nominations and the "best picture" Oscar – despite its initial X rating from the MPAA – while the reception of Warhol's film was quite the opposite. Critics panned it, and the FBI condemned it as perverse and dangerous, seizing it repeatedly during screenings in major cities throughout the early 1970s. Warhol's hopes of releasing the film to a large audience eventually died under the weight of government censorship and after its initial theatrical release, the film's distribution was limited to one small production run of VHS tapes in Britain. It had to be recovered for archival research purposes in a mid-1980s special joint project by the Museum of Modern Art and the Whitney Museum.

Lonesome Cowboys, with its vision of a gay frontier that is willing to reject John Wayne machismo, was noticeably less nostalgic in tone than *Midnight Cowboy*. That militancy was likely difficult for audiences to accept (when coupled with an avant-garde, art-house style that makes the film seem unpolished, disjointed, and inaccessible for many mainstream viewers). The contrasting success of *Midnight Cowboy* suggests how deeply it resonated with critics and audiences across the nation: though in many ways a far more depressing film, it interrogated cowboy masculinity while still valuing it. Joe's comment, "You're gonna tell me John Wayne's a fag?!", reveals an anxiety that mourned what was lost and tried desperately to cling to the cowboy myth despite its faltering. The Vietnam war and 1960s protest culture helped make *Midnight Cowboy* and *Lonesome Cowboys* possible, yet even at this watershed moment Americans were more receptive to a depressing dystopia as long as it properly mourned the erosion of the John Wayne myth. To Warhol's less depressing but far more seditious and liberating vision of a gay frontier, Americans responded with angry accusations of perversity.

In 1969, five years before Wayne blustered into Harvard Square, the stormy winds that had blown throughout the decade finally coalesced into a typhoon of change, engulfing and uprooting the myths of manhood upon which America had come to rely. Stepping out of the celluloid closet more decisively than ever before, the gay cowboy found himself at a crossroads. His future was still uncertain. The clear emergence of latent homoerotic subcurrents, and the shift beyond this newly apparent liminal space – appropriately, the genre's midnight hour – would continue after 1969, through to Lee's *Brokeback Mountain*. But the place of the gay cowboy within the larger matrix of American identity had begun to shift as he staked out a more visible space on the imagined frontier.

Notes

1. *Midnight Cowboy* has elements of gross homophobia. The comment "that [cowboy] stuff is for fags" is one of several derogatory comments. The first time that Rizzo meets Joe, he yells "get away faggot!" at an effeminate man who wanders up to their table. As far as "real" homosexuals are displayed in the movie, they usually exhibit severe self-loathing and are coded as pathetic or sinister. In some ways, *Midnight Cowboy* can be considered more homophobic than the westerns it deconstructs, as if it is compensating for the Pandora's box of masculine crisis that it helped to open. Though it was revolutionary for interrogating constructions of cowboy masculinity, the film seems deeply ambivalent over the answers it finds.
2. During his visit to Harvard, one student asked Wayne what he thought of the women's liberation movement, to which the star replied: "I think they have a right to work anywhere they want to [long pause] as long as they have dinner ready when we want it." And during his infamous 1971 interview with *Playboy*, Wayne remarked: "I don't feel we did wrong in taking this great country away from them [Native Americans]. Our so-called stealing of this country from them was just a matter of survival. There were great numbers of people who needed new land, and the Indians were selfishly trying to keep it for themselves."
3. Warhol also uses a rape scene to connect his cowboy story to the Vietnam war. One of the brothers in *Lonesome Cowboys* comments that the rape of Ramona "was fun," and another retorts: "we're not here for fun – we're here to... get ready for World War One." Playing cowboy like American GIs, the brothers' attack is seemingly a preparation for war. Yet the rape scene, during which Ramona yells "you faggots," is farcical, confirming – like *Midnight Cowboy* – the vulnerability of America's cowboy dreams and perhaps also the failure of its attempt at imperialist rape. Both films echo the emasculation of Kovic, crippled by a war wound, whose veteran memoir spoke of an invalid nation.

Works Cited

Bederman, Gail. *Manliness and Civilization*. Chicago: U of Chicago P, 1995.

Bird, Thomas. "Man and Boy Confront the Images of War." *New York Times* 27 May 1990, sec. 2: 11, 16.

Cole, Shaun. "Macho Men: Clones and the Development of a Masculine Stereotype." *Fashion Theory* 4.2 (2000): 125-40.

Elison, Bruce. Forum on "Human Rights in the United States: The Unfinished Story." 14 September 2000. National Archives and Records Administration.

Finch, Mark. "Lonesome Cowboys and Gay Cinema." *Andy Warhol Film Factory*. Ed. Michael O'Pray. London: British Film Institute, 1989.

68

Friedan, Betty. *The Feminine Mystique*. 1963. New York: Norton, 2001.

Hawks, Howard and Arthur Rosson, dirs. *Red River*. United Artists, 1948.

Herr, Michael. *Dispatches*. 1977. New York: Knopf, 1997.

Kellogg, Ray, John Wayne and Mervyn LeRoy, dirs. *The Green Berets*. Warner Bros., 1968.

Kifner, John. "John Wayne Plays a New Role: The Invader of Harvard Square." *New York Times* 16 January 1974: 41.

Kovic, Ron. *Born on the Fourth of July*. New York: McGraw, 1976.

Kubrick, Stanley, dir. *Full Metal Jacket*. Warner Bros., 1987.

Mahedy, William P. "It Don't Mean Nothin': The Vietnam War Experience." *The Vietnam Reader*. Ed. Walter Capps. New York: Routledge, 1991.

Major, Reginald. *A Panther is a Black Cat*. New York: W. Morrow, 1971.

Newton, Huey. "Executive Mandate Number One." 2 May 1967. *To Die for the People*. New York: Random House, 1972.

Pumphrey, Martin. "Why Do Cowboys Wear Hats in the Bath? Style Politics for the Older Man." *Critical Quarterly* 31.3 (1989): 78-100.

Rich, Adrienne. "Twenty-One Love Poems." *The Dream of a Common Language: Poems 1974-1977*. New York: Norton, 1978.

Roberts, Randy, and James Olson. *John Wayne: American*. New York: The Free Press, 1995.

Schlesinger, John, dir. *Midnight Cowboy*. United Artists, 1969.

Sherwell, Phillip. "John Wayne Made Real Movies. There Ain't No Queer in Cowboy." *London Telegraph* 1 January 2006 <http://www.telegraph.co.uk/news/main.jhtml?xml=/news/2006/01/01/wbroke01.xml>.

Suid, Lawrence. *Guts and Glory*. Reading: Addison-Wesley, 1978.

Slotkin, Richard. *Gunfighter Nation: The Myth of the Frontier in Twentieth Century America*. New York: Atheneum, 1992.

Student Non-Violent Coordinating Committee. "Statement on Vietnam, January 6, 1966." Black Protest: History, Documents, and Analyses, 1619 to the Present. Ed. Joanne Grant. Greenwich, Connecticut: Fawcett, 1974.

Teal, Donn. *The Gay Militants: How Gay Liberation Began in America*. New York: Stein and Day, 1971.

Voices from Wounded Knee, 1973, In the Words of the Participants. Rooseveltown: Akwesasne Notes, 1974.

Warhol, Andy, dir. *Lonesome Cowboys*. Sherpix, 1969.

Wayne, John. "Candid Conversation." *Playboy* May 1971: 75-92.

White, Water. "From Harrisburg, Pennsylvania." *Life* 19 December 1969: 46.

Wittman, Carl. "Refugees from Amerika: A Gay Manifesto." *American Protest Literature*. Ed. Zoe Trodd. Cambridge, MA: Harvard UP, 2006.

4

The Plagues of Egypt in the Promised Land:
Paul Thomas Anderson's *Magnolia*

Karl Martin

Structuralist literary critics have called our attention to metaphors that convey meaning primarily by establishing ideas in binary opposition to each other. We may have been taught to value good over evil, but we have also learned to define good primarily in relationship to evil. Students of racism and sexism have explored the ways such binary oppositions work in cultural definitions of white and black and male and female. Typically, "Each binary operation can be pictured as a fraction, the top half (the numerator) being what is more valued than its related bottom half (the denominator)" (Bressler 66). But, of course, such binary operations can be inverted and may then display that the concept "male" has no meaning aside from the concept "female." This act of the deconstruction of the binary operation allows us to see the two terms in a much more symbiotic relationship with each other. In other words, by looking at the way the term "male" relies for its cultural authority on the term "female," we can gain fresh perspective on the very category "male." The artificial nature of the categories is more easily seen when the binary is reversed.

Consider the metaphors associated with America – some of which predate even the era of exploration: "The New World," "The Promised Land," "Canaan," "The New Israel." All such terms function primarily in relationship to their binary opposites. Once we identify America as "The New Israel," for example, we call forth images of (and invite comparison to) Egypt or perhaps Babylon. If America is a Promised Land, then, by definition, it cannot be Egypt or Babylon. The existence of these binary oppositional terms allows those who criticize the idea that America is a New Israel to argue that the experiences of some Americans actually more closely resembles experiences of people in bondage in Egypt or in exile in

Babylon. We might think of spirituals such as "Go Down, Moses" that invert the fraction and identify some aspect of the American experience with Egyptian captivity. Or we might think of the frequent reference to some aspect of the American experience as time spent in Babylon that is prevalent in reggae music. In these cases, the particulars experienced by some local population are used to critique the abstract typological claims. America cannot be a New Israel if life in America resembles life in Egypt or Babylon.

In *Death of a Nation*, David W. Noble writes of the breakdown of what he identifies as "the aesthetic authority of bourgeois nationalism" that has been occurring in the United States since the forties (xxvii). Noble suggests that the metaphor of two worlds, of an old, corrupt Europe and the New World of America – held in binary opposition – has been eroding in recent decades. However, it has been challenged not to be discarded but to be replaced when its adherents can no longer reconcile a belief in the existence of the sacred space of the American nation alongside the belief in the sacred space of the international market required by their commitment to international capitalism. A more radical – and much less frequent – reaction is to relinquish a belief in the possibility of a timeless, unbounded Promised Land.

Noble's work is essential for this study, for he demonstrates the power of the metaphor of the New World and the importance of breaking its authority if we are to imagine a world different from the world dominated by either bourgeois nationalism or international capitalism. By surrendering the metaphors associated with national sacred space, we can call into question the idea of the international market as a sacred space as well because we call into question the very category of sacred space, of a human society or condition that has somehow transcended the ebb and flow of history and has become, instead, the telos of history. That is, we can argue against the possibility of the existence of sacred space in a fallen world. Rather than exchange one Promised Land – the nation state – for another – the international market, we might be empowered to relinquish a belief in sacred space altogether when we relinquish the sacred space of the national.

In an earlier study, one to which Noble owes a debt, Sacvan Bercovitch analyzed the narratives of American artists in the middle of the nineteenth century who, unable to relinquish their attachment to the sacred space of bourgeois nationalism, lose hope in hope itself. "When they abandoned their faith in America," Bercovitch writes in *The American Jeremiad*,

> they had no other recourse. The result was what we might call the anti-jeremiad: the denunciation of all ideals, sacred and secular, on the grounds that America is a lie.... In this country, both the jeremiad and the anti-jeremiad foreclosed alternatives: the one by absorbing the hopes of mankind into the meaning of America, the other by reading into America the futility and fraud of hope itself. (191)

Throughout the twentieth century, Bercovitch argues, narratives that first appeared to be radical critiques of bourgeois nationalism were actually absorbed into the mainstream culture. America's inability to live up to its promise was critiqued in the name of those very promises. He explains, "In post-industrial countries the tension between social structures and social ideals has usually been mediated by competing systems of values" (204). In the United States, the social ideal is so strong, so all-consuming, that competing values are rarely heard. "In this country," Bercovitch writes, "the *unmediated* relation between social structure and social ideal has made the very exposure of social flaws part of the ritual of socialization – a sort of liminal interior dialogue that in effect reinforces the mainstream culture" (204-5). In short, America is often criticized from the perspective of its failure to be as American as it should be. The inversion of the New Israel/Egypt binary may offer a way out of his rhetorical trap, for it has at its disposal the particulars of history – of lived experience brought into focus by the inversion of the binary – as a resource to judge the reality of American life without bringing into play the promise of America. In other words, the inversion allows for the criticism that the Promised Land is Egypt rather than the criticism that the Promised Land is not living up to its promise. In the latter, the promise is affirmed even while the failure is named. In the former, it is rejected.

In the popular culture of recent years, no one has more effectively inverted the New World/Old World, Israel/Egypt binary opposition – thereby implicitly challenging the metaphor of America as a New World – than does writer and director Paul Taylor Anderson in his 1999 film, *Magnolia*. Anderson's primary work, it seems, is that of dismantling the entrenched metaphor, of shattering the remnants of the aesthetic authority of bourgeois nationalism. The film forcefully portrays contemporary

American life as a form of bondage rather than the life of God's chosen ones lived in the promised land of a New Israel. While the film is filled with angry and hurting characters who spend the vast majority of their time lashing out at each other, the narrative of the film, I will argue, is ultimately hopeful. For by disrupting competing narratives, it creates the cultural space for the expression of a narrative of authentic hope and the expression of the true nature of our despair.

In the language of Old Testament theologian Walter Brueggemann – and perhaps only an Old Testament theologian can lead us through Anderson's final act – prophetic criticizing must precede prophetic energizing. Brueggemann argues that we live in a culture that encourages numbness, especially numbness about suffering and death – after all, if we are suffering in the land of promise, we have no one to truly blame but ourselves. Thus we live in a state of denial, denial that things are really as bad as they appear to be, as bad as our own personal experiences and the experiences of others confirm them to be at times. To offer prophetic criticism, a work of art must first "*offer symbols* that are adequate to the horror and massiveness of the experience which evokes numbness and requires denial" (49, emphasis in original unless noted). Secondly, the work must "*bring to public expression those very fears and terrors* that have been denied so long and suppressed so deeply that we do not know they are there" (50). Finally, a work of prophetic criticism must "*speak metaphorically but concretely about the real deathliness that hovers over us and gnaws within us,* and . . . speak neither in rage nor in cheap grace, but with the candor born of anguish and passion" (50).

Magnolia functions as a work of prophetic criticism by giving voice to the pain and suffering experienced by a remarkable group of characters whose lives intersect through one long day and night in Los Angeles. Anderson's intentional use of biblical material, specifically the plagues of Egypt, inverts the New Israel/Egypt binary opposition to encourage his audience to surrender the metaphor of America as a New World and to get his audience to, in the words of the Aimee Mann song used very effectively in the film, "Wise Up."

Before the primary action of the film, a voice-over narration tells three stories. The first tells of the murder of a man in the Greenberry Hill neighborhood of London in the early years of the twentieth century. The man is killed by three vagrants – men with the surnames Green, Berry, and Hill. The second story tells of a casino employee in Las Vegas who, while scuba diving in a lake, is scooped up by a fire-fighting plane as the plane transports water to a forest fire. The diver dies of a heart attack somewhere between the lake and being released above the fire. The pilot of the plane, who had played blackjack at the diver's table just two nights before, is unable to deal with the guilt of his unintended actions and kills himself shortly after the events. In the third story, we learn of a young man who attempts to commit suicide by jumping from the roof of the building in which he lives with his always-quarreling parents because he simply can no longer handle the fighting. The attempted suicide is a failure, for the young man lands in a safety net installed by window washers a few days earlier. The young man dies, nevertheless, for he is struck by a shotgun blast fired by his own mother who is quarrelling with his father. The blast misses his father but shatters the window and happens to strike the young man as he falls past the window. The final irony of the story is that, according to the testimony of a young boy in the building, the young man himself loaded the shotgun. He told the young boy that he hoped one of his parents would succeed in killing the other in their next quarrel. The stories sound very much like urban legends, yet the voiceover narration insists on their veracity and even cites seemingly credible news sources for each story. The overall message given by the narrator is that such events happen all the time – we simply refuse to acknowledge their existence, or as Brueggemann might say, we have become numb to them. The opening section provides a crucial narrative frame to the interrelated stories that are to follow and is invoked again at the end of Anderson's long film. The framing device, however, functions in an even more significant way, for it uses the particular experiences of individuals, taken from local settings, to challenge our common assumptions about how the world functions. In other words, our experience of the initial narrative frame disrupts our entrenched understanding of life as it is lived in a world ruled by reason and rationality and prepares us to listen and grant authority to the lived experiences of the characters we are about to meet, characters whose experiences mark them as living not in a Promised Land but in captivity in Egypt.

All of the action in a series or inter-related storylines takes place in one day in Southern California. None of the stories that follow, however, are relayed consecutively; rather, they are spliced together with jump cuts moving us from scene to scene, often at a frantic pace.

TV producer Earl "Big Earl" Partridge (the late Jason Robards) is terminally ill – his death from cancer is imminent. He is being cared for by Phil Parma (Philip Seymour Hoffman), a male nurse. When they are alone

one day, Partridge tells Parma that he has a son from whom he has been estranged since he abandoned the boy when his son was a teenager. Partridge walked out on his son and his first wife when she was dying of cancer, leaving the boy to care for his dying mother.

Partridge's son is the incredibly misogynistic motivational speaker Frank T.J. Mackey (Tom Cruise) who offers dating seminars for men entitled "Seduce and Destroy." At Partridge's request, Parma attempts to contact Mackey to tell him of his father's illness and the old man's wish to see him. Parma is finally able to contact Mackey (interrupting an interview with a journalist confronting Mackey with the truth about the past Mackey has worked very hard to conceal) and convince him to see his father before the old man dies. Partridge is incoherent by the time Mackey arrives; nevertheless, Mackey pours out his anger and his hurt in one of the film's most moving scenes. Partridge dies shortly after this visit from his son.

Partridge's second wife, Linda (Julianne Moore), is not handling her husband's impending death well at all. She confesses that she did not love Earl when she married him – she married him for his money – and confesses that she has cheated on him on numerous occasions. Yet now, in Partridge's illness, she has truly fallen in love with him. She even goes to the family lawyer and asks to be taken out of his will in an attempt to punish herself for her infidelity to Partridge. When she can finally no longer deal with Earl's illness, she leaves him in the hands of Parma and takes an overdose of prescription medication in her car. She is discovered by a young black boy (played by the appropriately named Emmanuel Johnson), who appears several times in the film, and he calls the paramedics. The last time we see her she is in a hospital bed, apparently recovering from her suicide attempt.

Meanwhile, we meet Jimmy Gator (Philip Baker Hall), quizmaster of a program called *What Do Kids Know?*, a Big Earl Partridge Production. Gator is also dying from cancer and is trying to reconcile with his daughter, Claudia (Melora Walters), who wants nothing to do with him. She explodes in anger when he arrives at her apartment and wakes her up in her bedroom to speak with her. After collapsing and barely making it through an episode of the quiz show he hosts, Gator goes home to his wife, Rose (Melinda Dillon). He confesses to her that he has been unfaithful in their marriage. She presses the issue by asking why their daughter is so angry with him. He tells Rose that Claudia – a cocaine addict so desperate for a fix that she trades sex for drugs – believes he sexually molested her when she was young. When Rose asks Jimmy if he actually did molest their daughter, he can only say that he does not remember, that he cannot say. Rose insists that he does know and will not say. Following her husband's quasi-confession, Rose goes to be with Claudia, and Jimmy goes to the kitchen and gets a gun; he is contemplating suicide.

The character who holds these multiple storylines together somewhat is police officer Jim Kurring (John C. Reilly). When we first meet him, he is in the apartment of a very distressed woman named Marcie (Cleo King) who is trying to keep him from discovering the dead man in her bedroom closet as he asks her questions about her son and grandson, who may be implicated in the man's death. Kurring handles the situation as calmly as possible. Before leaving the scene, he is confronted by the same young black boy (probably Marcie's grandson although this is not finally confirmed by the film) who will later assist Linda; he promises to help solve the case by performing a rap for the policeman. In the rap, the boy proclaims himself a prophet and tells Kurring, "When the sunshine don't work / The good Lord bring the rain in." Because he cannot make sense of it, the text of the rap challenges Kurring's ability to keep the world of experience under rational control, challenges his ability, as an officer of the law with a nightstick and a holster holding a gun, to provide stability to the people he encounters. The rap also foreshadows two scenes. The first is the driving rainstorm during which Kurring is shot at by a murder suspect implied to be Marcie's son and during which he loses his gun. The second is the film's most dramatic visual moment – when "the good Lord" brings in a rain of frogs as a judgment on all that has occurred.

Later in the day, officer Kurring is called to Claudia's apartment because of a noise complaint. An honest, hard working officer prone to talking to himself about the challenges of his job, Kurring is immediately smitten with Claudia – even though she is strung out when they meet. Kurring asks Claudia out on a date and plans to return that evening to pick her up. Before he returns, Kurring loses his gun. A large contingent of police is called out to help search for the gun but cannot find it. The audience knows that the mysterious young rapper – the same boy who calls the paramedics for Linda and announces the coming rain – picks it up. Kurring feels humiliated by what he considers to be a terrible failure on his part. He, nevertheless, returns to pick up Claudia for their date. The date is marked by awkwardness, but both Jim and Claudia are clearly hungry for relationship. Claudia pledges to tell Jim the full truth about herself, and Jim agrees to do the same. Jim demonstrates his commitment by telling Claudia about his failed marriage and the loss of his gun. Claudia, fearing that Jim cannot possibly love her in her current state, cannot tell him the truth and hides from her date her cocaine addiction and the sexual abuse she is trying so hard to avoid confronting. She cuts the date short and returns home to her cocaine. The date is the clearest example of the claim put forth by Brueggemann that we live in a society that discourages us from telling the truth about our experiences, especially our experiences of suffering, loss, and death. While Jim is able to speak the truth to Claudia, she cannot reciprocate. Claudia attempts to overcome this tendency but cannot, at least not yet.

Earlier in the day, Jimmy Gator taped an episode of *What Do Kids Know?* featuring a boy-genius named Stanley Spector (Jeremy Blackman). Stanley is on the verge of leading his team, consisting of himself and two other children, to record winnings on *What Do Kids Know?* But Stanley is not happy with his conquests in large part because he is being used by his father as a meal ticket. The abusive Mr. Spector (Michael Bowen) is also hoping to build on Stanley's show business connections to launch an acting career of his own. In a painful scene to witness, Stanley pees his pants when he is not allowed to go to the bathroom during a commercial break at the show's taping. As a result of this accident, Stanley is unwilling to stand and take his place as his team's representative for the final round of the quiz. His refusal incurs the wrath of his father and the quiz show officials.

One of the most interested viewers of Stanley's assault on the quiz show record is Quiz Kid Donnie Smith (played with great pathos by William H. Macy). Now an adult, Smith still holds the all time record for winnings on the program and continues to attempt to make a living by cashing in on his minor and fading celebrity. Smith has fallen on very hard times. All of the money he earned on the quiz show was taken from him and spent by his parents. In a series of scenes, we see Smith inadvertently driving his car through the window of a mini-mart, being fired from his job as the spokesman for an electronics company, unsuccessfully attempting to pick up a male bartender, breaking in to the safe at his former employer's store, and finally attempting to break back into the store in order to put back the money he has stolen.

Jim Kurring, returning from his date with Claudia, sees Donnie Smith attempting to break into the electronics store and decides to investigate. Meanwhile, Rose is on her way to comfort Claudia who is at home snorting cocaine, Jimmy Gator is holding a gun to his head, Linda is being transported to the hospital by paramedics, Phil Parma and Frank T.J. Mackey are with Big Earl in the final moments of his life, and Stanley sits serenely studying.

At this point, in one of the most initially inexplicable scenes in the history of American movies, frogs begin to fall from the sky.

The preceding plot summary of the film feels inadequate, not because it is inaccurate but because it is misleading regarding the tone of the film. None of the stories is told in chronological order. Rather, Anderson creates a pastiche through repeated jump cuts from storyline to storyline. The overall message, nevertheless, is clear. The world of *Magnolia* is a world filled with chaos and many angry, damaged, hurting, or cruel people, and none of the victims seems able to give adequate or full voice to his or her suffering and grief. The first part of the film is filled with scene after scene depicting the disregard characters feel for one another, a disregard conveyed to the audience through the profanity-laced dialogue of nearly every character except Jim Kurring and Phil Parma. To provide just one example, while watching his son compete on *What Do Kids Know?*, Rick Spector, father of contestant and whiz-kid Stanley, is comparing notes with the other stage parents. They are speaking of the difficulty they have in disciplining their very bright and much celebrated children. Spector tells them, "You have to be subtly abusive so they don't know what's happening." In contrast to Spector's strategy, many of the characters make no attempt to make their abuse subtle.

These scenes of abuse in the film seem to finally play themselves out – more than two hours into the film – as Aimee Mann's "Wise Up" plays, and each of the primary characters sings along in turn. The lyrics read:

> It's not / What you thought /
> When you first began it / You got /
> What you want / Now you can hardly stand it, though /
> By now you know / It's not going to stop /
> It's not going to stop / It's not going to stop /
> 'Til you wise up
>
> You're sure / There's a cure /
> And you have finally found it / You think /
> One drink / Will shrink you 'til you're underground /
> And living down / But it's not going to stop /

> It's not going to stop / It's not going to stop /
> 'Til you wise up
>
> Prepare a list of what you need /
> Before you sign away the deed /
> 'Cause it's not going to stop / It's not going to stop /
> No it's not going to stop / 'Til you wise up
>
> No it's not going to stop / 'Til you wise up /
> No it's not going to stop / So just give up.

The final voice is that of Stanley, the vulnerable current star of *What Do Kids Know?* The hopeless call to "just give up" is, thankfully, not the film's last word.

The final indication that the film is addressing issues of national identity and not merely trying to portray scenes of contemporary life comes near the end of the film when, as I have stated, frogs begin to fall from the sky. Few viewers in the theater could have been ready for this scene, but those of us who have had the luxury of repeated viewings of the film on DVD can better understand Anderson's strikingly odd cinematic vision. What we learn is that we have been carefully prepared for this final shocking scene well in advance.

As Jimmy Gator prepares for the taping of *What Do Kids Know?*, the cameraman pans the audience. On one aisle a fan holds up a sign reading "Go Stanley." On the other aisle a man holds a sign reading "Exodus 8:2." While this is an obvious satire of the ubiquitous "John 3:16" signs at sporting events, it carries textual significance as well. Exodus 8:2 reads, "But if you refuse to let them go, behold, I will smite your whole territory with frogs." This sign is not the first reference to the Exodus text. Prior to the first scene of this eventful day, viewers are given a weather report. We are told that there will be an 82% chance of rain; this provides a further link to the Exodus text as the reference 8:2 becomes 82%. In addition, when we first see Jim Kurring in his home, we hear the text of a message callers receive when they call a dating service with whom he has registered. His box number is given as 82. And Donnie Smith makes reference to Exodus in a scene in a bar. Talking to himself, he quotes a line from Shakespeare saying, "The sins of the father laid upon the children" and then notes that the passage is "borrowed from Exodus 20:5." That the deluge of frogs is associated with judgment is confirmed in the words of the rap delivered to Officer Kurring – it is the "good Lord" who is bringing the rain.

The linkage of the Exodus text with Stanley established at the taping of the television program is very important, for it provides the connection to an even more significant Egyptian plague – the deaths of the first born in all of Egypt. This connection becomes clear when we begin to consider the various family trees featured in the film. As far as we know, except for Claudia, who appears to be the oldest child of Jimmy and Rose Gator, none of the *Magnolia* families have more than one child; thus, every child in these families is the firstborn. And they have all been damaged by actions taken by their parents.

Quiz Kid Donnie Smith tells us that his parents took and spent all of the money he made as a quiz show contestant. He is left with nothing to show for his early brilliance except the fading celebrity he repeatedly attempts to exploit in both personal and business relationships. Stanley Spector is being used by his father as both a meal ticket and as a potential trailblazer for his own entry into show business. The constant harassment by the father culminates in Stanley feeling so intimidated that he cannot even assert his right to use the restroom when he desperately needs to during the taping. Even after he has peed in his pants trying to please his father and the other adults in his world, he receives no sympathy from his abusive father.

Motivational speaker Frank T.J. Mackey, easily the angriest person in the film – he does, after all, run the dating seminar "Seduce and Destroy" – is abandoned by his father when he is only an adolescent, abandoned at a time when his mother is dying of cancer. Left to care for his mother alone, Mackey has never been able to forgive his father, not that his father has ever sought his forgiveness. We are shown scenes from an interview between a television journalist and Mackey. When the journalist questions the account of his life made available to the public through official press material and confronts Mackey with the truth of his past, the loquacious Mackey retreats into silence. Shortly after this interview, the nurse attending Earl Partridge succeeds in getting through to Mackey and telling him of his father's impending death and Earl's desire to see his son before he dies. Mackey arrives but remains filled with rage and is un-reconciled to his father.

That Mackey's anger is rooted in this deep hurt is revealed in one of the most powerful scenes in the film, when Frank comes to his father's deathbed. The scene is not a scene of reconciliation, for Earl Partridge is not even coherent; rather, it is a scene of catharsis as Mackey is finally able to express the root of his anger towards the world. He is able finally to give voice to the pain of his own experience. In the words of Brueggemann, he is able to speak "with the candor born of anguish and passion" (50).

If Mackey is the angriest of the firstborns, Claudia Gator is clearly the most deeply damaged. Claudia never appears in a scene while sober. She is so addicted to cocaine that she snorts coke while a police officer is in the next room of her apartment. She gets high both before and after a date with Officer Kurring, who truly seems to care for her. When we first meet her, she is prostituting herself in trade for cocaine. That Claudia's addiction is rooted in her relationship with her father is made clear when he enters the bedroom in her apartment and wakes her to try and tell her he is dying. She explodes in anger, repeatedly challenging him to once again call her a "whore."

As mentioned above, in a later scene, Jimmy Gator admits to his wife that he cannot remember whether or not he abused their daughter Claudia. Late in the film, viewers are given confirmation of the abuse during a brief close up of a painting hanging near Claudia's front door. In the corner of the frame, a typed message has been attached to the painting that reads, "but it did happen." Claudia is portrayed as a woman who has been debilitated by guilt and self-hatred rooted in the sexual abuse committed against her by her father and made worse by her inability to voice that deep hurt.

We have moved from Exodus 8 to Exodus 11 – the plague of the deaths of the firstborn sons of all of Egypt – and we witness a specific binary reversal. These Americans are not Israelites held in captivity but Egyptian oppressors. They will not be passed over during this last plague. The Passover is arguably the centerpiece of Jewish identity. Anderson's use of it in the film marks the clear reversal of the Promised Land/Egypt binary operation. To make matters even worse, this plague does not rain down from some all-powerful deity on the beloved children of a people guilty of oppressing others; rather, this plague is visited on the children by their own parents.

Through all of this chaos walks one remarkably calm man -- Officer Jim Kurring. Flawed himself – Kurring is divorced – he remains committed to doing good in any way he possibly can. Kurring is prone to talking to himself, so we often hear his reflections on his job and his role in the world. We first meet him as he responds to a domestic disturbance call, and we watch as he remains remarkably calm in the presence of a very angry woman who is trying to keep him from discovering the dead body in the closet of her bedroom. Kurring's next encounter will prove even more revealing of his character.

During a driving rainstorm, Kurring is called to Claudia's apartment by neighbors complaining about the noise – Claudia is so strung out that she has no idea how loud her music is blaring. Certainly aware that Claudia is high, Jim, nevertheless, does not arrest her. In fact, he is smitten with her from the moment he first sees her. He nearly leaves before saying anything. As he stands in the hallway, wondering whether he should again knock on her door, he drops his nightstick, foreshadowing the loss of his service revolver. He finally decides to return and ask her for a date. They arrange to meet for dinner that night. As Kurring drives away, he makes a promise to God saying, "And God, I'm telling you right now, I will not screw it up. You gave me an opportunity. I'm going to treat this young lady right."

Before the afternoon is over, Kurring loses his gun while pursuing a suspect – most likely Marcie's son. We see the young rapper pick up the weapon and leave the area, but Kurring does not. He searches for his weapon while praying desperately to God for help. At one point in his prayer, he admits to God, "I'm lost out here." Without his gun, he believes he has lost his ability to do good in the world. But the loss of his weapon, like the earlier dropping of his nightstick, is an important symbolic act. As a police officer, Kurring is an agent of the state. In the symbolic world Anderson has created, he is an Egyptian overseer charged with keeping the oppressed slaves in line. Stripped of the symbol of his authority, Kurring goes into the long night vulnerable. Perhaps in this state he can more adequately help those in immediate need. And this loss of his authority occurs during a driving rainstorm, the significance of which has been established by the young rapper who earlier proclaimed, "When the sunshine don't work / The good Lord brings the rain in." The identification of God as the source of the rain may indicate that God needs to strip Officer Kurring of the assumed authority of the state before he can be empowered to be an effective agent of real change in the lives of other characters.

The prayer Kurring prays for help in finding his gun does not receive an immediate answer, and he is forced to admit to his superiors that he has lost his weapon and to call in help for the search to recover it. As a consequence of his loss, Kurring goes to dinner with Claudia at his most vulnerable. He is not only out of uniform, he is an officer without his service revolver. Jim's vulnerability allows him to make a connection with Claudia but keeps him from being able to offer her the stability and protection he believes she needs, security and protection symbolized by his weapon – itself a symbol of Kurring's role as an agent of state authority. Instead, he is able to speak of the deep hurt he has experienced, to give voice to his suffering, and he is able to allow Claudia to speak as well. At that moment, Claudia is still too damaged to risk such speech, but Kurring's relationship to her is no longer as an agent of state authority hoping to bring order to chaos. He is now relating to her as one wounded and needy person to another. This relationship foreshadows Kurring's relationship to Quiz Kid Donnie Smith.

The final act of the film begins as Kurring is driving home following his date, when he witnesses Smith attempting to climb to the roof of an electronics store to break in and, ironically, return to the store's safe the money he has previously stolen. Before examining this last scene, we need to spend some time with Quiz Kid Donnie Smith. Smith is easily the most pathetic character in the film. Surely Frank and Claudia have experienced more significant losses in their lives, but neither dwells on the loss with quite the same passion as Donnie. Claudia buries her hurt in her addiction, and Mackey compensates with bluster. Quiz Kid Donnie Smith simply rehashes the pain and suffering.

Through a number of his scenes, we learn that Smith is attempting to get braces in a futile attempt to impress a male bartender on whom he has a crush. The bartender barely knows Donnie is alive and is unimpressed with his fading celebrity status. Attempting to get closer to the bartender, Donnie strikes up a conversation with a homosexual barfly named, of all things, Thurston Howell (played with wonderful subtlety by Henry Gibson). As the new quiz show featuring Stanley runs on the bar television, Donnie and Howell exchange cryptic conversation. At one point, the barfly tells Donnie, "It is a dangerous thing to confuse children with angels." Following his embarrassing confession of love for the bartender, Donnie goes into the men's room to vomit, but not before announcing, "And the book says we may be through with the past, but the past is not through with us" (a line heard earlier from Jimmy Gator). The "book" here should be seen as the Bible, for Donnie will soon call our attention to Exodus chapter 20, which describes how pain is passed down through generations. Smith goes on to contradict Howell by saying, "No, it is not a dangerous thing to confuse children with angels." It is while hunched over the toilet that he begins to recite the line from Shakespeare that he identifies as coming from Exodus 20. The full commandment reads: "You shall not worship them or serve them; for I, the Lord your God, am a jealous God visiting the iniquity of the fathers on the children, on the third and fourth generations of those who hate Me" (Exodus 20:5).

Still not able to regain control over his life, Donnie is next seen as he decides to break into the safe at his former employer's store. He steals the money and leaves the store, but as he is locking the outer door, the key breaks off in the lock. As he is driving away, Donnie finally realizes just how pathetic he has become. He decides to return the money to the store, but when he approaches the door he realizes that the key is broken in the lock. He decides to climb to the roof and break into the building. It is at this point that Jim sees Donnie and decides to investigate.

It is also at this point that the plague of the frogs begins. Character after character is shown in stances ranging from amazement to panic. Jimmy Gator's suicide attempt is spoiled when a frog, falling through a sky-light, causes the gun he is pointing at his head to discharge into the screen of a nearby television (the film then suggests that an electrical fire may begin at any moment and claim Gator's life in the ensuing house fire). Perhaps inspired by the wonder of what he sees, Stanley finally confronts his father, negating the despair suggested in the lyrics of "Wise Up." He wakes his father with his repeated demand: "Dad, you need to be nicer to me." In characteristic fashion, Jim Kurring thinks of others rather than himself. He ventures from the relative safety of his car to where Donnie has fallen to the street and drags Smith to safety. As they sit under cover at a gas station, a wonderful moment of grace occurs. Jim's gun falls from the sky in the midst of the frogs. Chastened and humbled by the earlier loss of his weapon, Kurring recovers the gun, but in his final act of compassion, he will not rely on the symbolic authority of the state as represented by the gun as he once did but will rather subsume his role as an agent of the state to his role as comforter and moral guide, rooting his judgment in whatever help people may need, not in the law but in his relationships with them.

Like a medieval knight in a grail legend, Jim Kurring has been restored to wholeness and can thus resume his duties, can resume bringing order to this chaos; however, he now clearly sides with those suffering. He decides not to arrest Donnie Smith but rather to allow him to return the money to the safe. And in the film's final scene, he has returned once again to attempt to establish a relationship with Claudia. Significantly,

Kurring's restoration occurs only after he has given voice to his pain and anguish over having lost his gun in a moment of honesty during his date with Claudia and after he has shown mercy to Donnie Smith.

With all of the abusive parents either dead or confronted, we can finally feel as though the plague has been lifted. The film's final image is a wonderful if weak smile on the lips of Claudia as Jim announces his intentions to court her. Perhaps now she will be able to speak the truth of her own experiences, acknowledging her pain rather than burying it in a mountain of cocaine.

Anderson's film attacks the metaphor of America as a new Promised Land in the only truly effective way possible, by dismantling the initial claim with his symbolic use of the Egyptian plagues, by challenging the belief in a chosen people, an elect nation. Attempting more gently to correct the understanding of the promise, generations of artists and reformers have ended up affirming its basic precepts. In other words, they have redefined but not renounced the promise of America, but, as Bercovitch has argued, they have been unable to dislodge the idea that America remains a Promised Land. If David Noble is correct, many Americans since World War II have not given up the idea of a Promised Land but have merely shifted the locus of the promise from the nation state to the international market. Rather than refining the nature of the promise, the reversal of the binary operation reveals the foolishness of the claim itself thereby stopping the transference of the promise from the nation state to the international marketplace by renouncing the promise itself. Simultaneously, the film shows that affirmation of America as a Promised Land is not needed in order for America to be seen as a place where love, hope, and redemption are possible. In fact, it is only when Jim Kurring's authority as an agent of the state is compromised in the midst of both a shower of raindrops and a rain of frogs that he can truly begin to address the needs of the wounded people he encounters.

Narratives of bourgeois nationalism, historically, have tended toward the appropriation of all other narratives for the cause of the nation. In the United States, for example, national leaders have routinely given voice to a form of civil religion that borrows the rhetoric of the Bible and the Christian church but strips the Gospel of its distinctive message, and thus its power, by suggesting that salvation can be found in the nation. As narratives of bourgeois nationalism have themselves been challenged by the narratives asserting the need to protect the sacred space of the international marketplace (narratives claiming that access to global markets is so sacred that whatever sacrifices must be made in the lives of people at the local level to protect the functioning of the international marketplace are appropriate), we should expect that those who, knowingly or unknowingly, defend the sacred space of international capitalism will attempt to appropriate the language of the Bible and the Christian church for their purposes just as earlier bourgeois nationalists have done. Works of art, such as Paul Taylor Anderson's *Magnolia*, that disrupt embedded narratives and speak the truth about human suffering can help create a space where people can live neither as God's chosen nor as their Egyptian oppressors. Rather, they can live in honesty, openness, and humility with one another, giving voice to the particular truths of their own experiences rather than denying those experiences in service of a false promise.

Work Cited

Anderson, Paul Thomas, dir. *Magnolia*. With Tom Cruise, Julianne Moore, John C. Reilly, William H. Macy, and Jason Robards. New Line Cinema, 1999.

Bercovitch, Sacvan. *The American Jeremiad*. Madison: U of Wisconsin P, 1978.

Bressler, Charles. *Literary Criticism: An Introduction to Theory and Practice*. Englewood Cliffs, NJ: Prentice Hall, 1994.

Brueggemann, Walter. *The Prophetic Imagination*. Philadelphia: Fortress, 1978.

Mann, Aimee. "Wise Up." Lyrics. *Magnolia: Music from the Motion Picture*. Warner Brothers, 1999.

Noble, David W. *Death of a Nation: American Culture and the End of Exceptionalism*. Minneapolis: U of Minnesota P, 2002.

86

5

Reifying Cold War (Sub)urban Systems:
The Spatial Anatomy of Black Masculinity in
A Raisin in the Sun

Michael P. Moreno

If suburbia became the representation of safety during the Cold War era, it concurrently came to signify the American Dream of success. For many middle-class white Americans in the 1950s, the ownership of single-family homes in the suburbs, away from the perceived suffocation of the urban-scape, functioned as "the most visible symbol of having arrived at a fixed place in society, the goal to which every *decent* family aspired. It was an investment many people hoped would provide a ticket to higher status and wealth" (Jackson 50, italics mine). Unlike the city, where personal space was thought to be confining and limiting, where the terrain of the public and the private were intimately inter-meshing, where the topography is often fixed and predetermined, suburbia seemed to provide a fresh start where the open expanse offered unlimited opportunities to carve one's mark and make one's space anew.

This "new space" became the American Dream reborn, a matrix of lifestyle and expression, the contemporary Manifest Destiny, a new occasion to redefine and redesign the American landscape. According to the ideal fostered during the 1950s, living in the suburbs would amalgamate home and family within the refuge of a homogeneous community. However, much of what we conceptualize today as *suburban*, and most of what is theorized or represented as the utopic ideal versus the dystopic disenchantment with this phenomenon, comes from our own mythologizing of this non-urban landscape. Throughout white middle-class America, the suburban narrative ensured a sense of prosperity and security. However, those who did not fit into the mold of the suburban ideal were relegated to the margins and rendered invisible and irrelevant. Elaine Tyler May writes, "Black Americans, as a result of institutionalized racism and widespread poverty, existed on the fringes of the middle-class family idea. Suburbia was not part of the [wider] black experience, since blacks were systematically excluded from postwar suburbs" (13). For black families, this containment policy restricted them to the panoptic parcels of the city, further disenfranchising them. This placed black men and women in the precarious position of downward mobility, while ensuring white masculinity as the dominant cultural discourse in the United States.

Lorraine Hansberry's play *A Raisin in the Sun* (1959) and its film adaptation (1961) produce crystalline snapshots of this new Cold War national order of masculinity in crisis. The fragmentation of American masculinity during the Cold War further underscores how suburbia functions as a heterotopic site that dismantles traditional and singular constructions and depictions of manhood while revealing, even generating, simultaneously colliding definitions of masculine social ordering in American culture. While males were being represented in Hollywood as urban intellectuals, the war heroes, the organization men, or the suburban consumer, Hansberry's male black protagonist, Walter Lee Younger, wrestles with his own self-images of the servant/chauffeur, urban entrepreneur, and suburban patriarch. The Cold War suburb is responsible for the death of the "traditional" male in American society and complicates masculinity by simultaneously generating alternative roles of the male that co-exist and collide in a heterotopic storm of power and disenfranchisement.

Whereas the white male was often recast from the early American cities' entrepreneurial figure to the postwar suburbs' organization man, the black male was denied this same transformation, prohibited via economic and educational sanctions from participating in the burgeoning mass market economy. Consequently, "it was the values of the white middle class that shaped the dominant political and economic institutions that affected all Americans. Those who did not conform to them [or were not permitted to do so] were likely to be marginalized, stigmatized, and disadvantaged as a result" (May 13). The identities and mobility of black American men were thus and perhaps once again relegated to a new but still servile position. Equally, many were tempted by the illusion of freedom offered by this new pioneer spirit of entrepreneurship that had remained ghost-like in the abandoned ghetto spaces of the old city.

This suburban American dream, so disparate from the urban realities of Cold War America, is what Walter Lee Younger clings to in Lorraine Hansberry's film adaptation of her play *A Raisin in the Sun* (1961). Walter Lee (Sidney Poitier), a working-class black man living in Chicago's Southside, yearns to prove to himself and his family that he can function as patriarch and provider by using his deceased father's life insurance payment to enter into a liquor store partnership with two of his friends. Although his mother Lena (Claudia McNeil) has designs to relocate to an inhospitable white suburb with her daughter Beneatha (Diana Sands), her daughter-in-law Ruth (Ruby Dee), and her grandson Travis (Stephan Perry), Walter sees the $10,000 windfall as his one and only opportunity to become an entrepreneur and empower himself as a successful black businessman within his urban community. However, despite the opportunistic appeal of being self-employed, Walter must abandon this dream of urban achievement for the postwar one of domesticity in the suburbs if he is to become a patriarch in a Cold War society.

There is a stage-like quality throughout the film, which is made deliberate by the lighting that casts characters' shadows against walls or the framing of key scenes. Hansberry herself developed the screenplay for the filmic adaptation and kept most of the same leading cast members as well. In doing so, Hansberry was able to sustain much of the Broadway finesse that made her play so popular when it initially opened in 1959. Additionally, Hansberry retained the majority of the play's original dialogue in her screenplay. As such, there was some "contention that *A Raisin in the Sun* [was] less a movie than a filmed stage play" (Marill 98) when the film was released by Columbia Pictures in 1961. Literally "filming" the play made Hansberry's dramatic work accessible to a much wider audience by taking "the average filmgoer into the grime and grit of the ghetto. It exposed the matriarchal set-up in black homes and examined the emasculation of the black male by a hostile white society" (Bogle 196). *Raisin*, then, becomes more than a testimony of "[t]he grave disappointments associated with the failure of Northern industrial urbanism to deliver on the promise of economic and social opportunity" to urban blacks (Rotella 99); it succinctly illustrates how black masculinity challenges and is challenged by white male hegemony, and how the fractured identity of the black male is rooted within a Cold War heterotopia of colliding masculine roles. Pitted against fantasies of urban success, working class imprisonment, and illusions of suburban liberation,

Walter Lee Younger struggles with defining his own masculine space within the Cold War African-American community.

Beneath the surface of Hansberry's award-winning play and film, which are based loosely on her own life experience, lies the story of the Youngers' problematic and differing desires in regards to upward and outward mobility. To recover his masculinity and sense of power, Walter Lee is made to believe he must relocate his family from the racial, economic, and spatial confines of their urban ghetto apartment to the domestic sphere of a suburban dwelling. However, in order to negotiate this passage successfully and transform his family into a nuclear one, he has to reject the world of urban entrepreneurship and conform to the domestication of his own masculinity by becoming a suburbanite. It is here, in this alternative space, that Walter Lee will function as new head-of-household, thus positioning all other female members into a site of subordination while breaching the homogenous topography of postwar America's suburban utopia. As such, *A Raisin in the Sun* filmically charts the black masculine figure from its urban mold of entrepreneurship to its illusory reconfiguration as suburban patriarch.

This radical call to hyper-masculinity was widely articulated by many black political voices during the time of the play's performance and filmic evolution. According to Eldridge Cleaver, one of the founding leaders of the Black Panther movement during the Cold War, it was the white male who had been historically responsible for the emasculation of the black American male: "Since the days of slavery...the white man had refused to allow the black man to fulfill his traditional role as a man, that is, to serve as his family's sole provider and protector. Rather, white male domination had delegated that responsibility to the black woman. In robbing the black man of his traditional role, the white man had deprived him 'of his masculinity, castrated him in the center of his burning skull'" (qtd. in Corber 49). It is from this cycle of social and historical violence that Walter Lee tries to escape, and it is this alleged world of freedom and mobility towards which he strives.

In the cramped confines of the Youngers' Chicago Southside apartment, a small kitchen window permits a view of the extending building and a neighbor's nearby fire escape/balcony, thus emphasizing the lack of privacy offered in these low-income, urban sectors. Accentuated by the film's black and white cinematography, the tiny rooms are dark and layered in sharp shadows, for "[t]he sole natural light the family may enjoy in the course of a day is only that which fights its way *through this little window*," according to the original play's stage directions (Hansberry 24). Intimate medium close-up shots of the apartment's inhabitants and visitors are ubiquitous throughout the film, underscoring the claustrophobia and anxiety exhibited by the characters, particularly Walter Lee's. The camera itself, at times, conveys the impression of spatial intrusion into the Youngers' Chicago home.

This mounting tension, created by the restrictions within this urban space, is evident in the film's opening breakfast scene that transpires between Walter Lee and his wife Ruth. With the insurance check en-route to the Younger household, Walter Lee has been scheming with two of his friends to open up a liquor store together somewhere in the neighborhood, much to the moral indignation of the other family members. Disconcerted by the matriarchal system that currently governs the home's domestic site, Walter Lee attempts to coax Ruth into coercing his mother, Lena, into believing that his business proposition is sound and viable. In the scene, he attempts to win Ruth over to his side by reminding her of the dream she herself harbors of escaping the ghetto: "You tired, ain't you? Tired of everything. Me, the boy, the way we live – this beat-up hole – everything. Ain't you?...but you wouldn't do nothing to help, would you?...Mama would listen to you" (*Raisin*). Although Walter Lee appears to be powerless through his perpetual pleading and soliciting, the camera angles frame him slightly from below, giving him a towering and arresting demeanor. By contrast, Ruth, who is disclosed as being the only one able to convince "Mama" that Walter Lee's dream of entrepreneurship is tenable, is framed with her back to the camera for the major duration of the exchange. The authority she is supposed to have residing in this matriarchy remains unconfirmed by the camera lens and by her objectified positioning on the stage-like set.

However, when the audience does see Ruth in reaction shots, the camera is angled down towards her to reveal her weak and tired frame, clearly eclipsed by Sydney Poitier's fluid and "almost choreographic floor pacing gyrations that convey...[his] inner turmoil" throughout the film (qtd. in Marill 99). Whereas Ruth's empowerment comes by way of Walter Lee's goading, Walter Lee is mobile and gesticulates melodramatically to ensure his filmic control over the scene as well as over Ruth's body. This viability and power assigned to a black male protagonist was considered innovative in early 1960s classic Hollywood cinema, for it ensured that the black male image would subjugate the black female counterpart. Although Hollywood replaced the traditional dominating white male character with a black body, it confirmed for the spectator that a woman, regardless of her class or ethnicity, was still the object of the male gaze. "The male protagonist," according to Laura Mulvey, "is free to command the stage, a stage of spatial illusion in which he articulates the look and creates the action" (28). Additionally, "through participation in [Walter Lee's] power, the spectator can indirectly possess [Ruth] too" (29), thereby completing the cycle of the on-screen black woman's "to-be-looked-at-ness" (27) and normalization of her passivity via the black male.

The kitchen-dining-living room functions as a site for castration anxiety, psychoanalytically speaking, where Walter Lee's masculinity is constantly challenged by the women who also inhabit this space. As the film progresses, Walter Lee's patience with his feminized family wanes, and his disquietude becomes more evident from his excessive drinking and incessant pacing throughout the apartment. Having heard Walter Lee's financial schemes before, Ruth goes through the motions of listening in this opening scene, yet remains remotely interested in what he has to say. "Eat your eggs" is her only response to his proposition as she stirs about the kitchen re-clenching her matronly bathrobe. This line is repeated by Ruth throughout the duration of the scene and is more resilient each time she delivers it, for "eat your eggs" epitomizes her desire to live out the life of a suburban housewife, a lifestyle that requires the mimicry of domesticated white women. More importantly, it symbolizes Ruth's fertility, for the audience learns later that she is with child, thus characterizing her as a female and a mother. The subtle and seemingly trite request juxtaposed against Walter Lee's desperate imploration asserts how she wishes to construct her identity and the architectural composition of her family.[1] Whereas white suburban housewives during the Cold War must constantly defer their dreams of escaping their confining, albeit privileged, suburban lifestyle to the cultural landscape of the city, Ruth still maintains that a life such as ones led by these privileged women is preferable to a life of poverty and anguish in a black ghetto. This is an identity that can only come into fruition outside of the confining ghetto-topography, yet it is a lifestyle Ruth has been forced to defer because of her family's financial circumstances and the cultural conditions for urban blacks during the Cold War. More significantly, Ruth's dream of a suburban existence is predicated on the illusion that life, liberty, and the pursuit of happiness are only possible through participating in the consumptive lifestyle of the suburbs.

The breakfast scene establishes the inner-family impasse between Walter Lee and Ruth/Lena, and by extension urban entrepreneurial drives and suburban desires for domestic security. However, a later scene – in which Lena rejects Walter Lee's proposal for investing the insurance money in a liquor store and then challenges his manhood over Ruth's decision to terminate her unexpected pregnancy – breaks this deadlock by dislocating Walter Lee from any position of respect or authority in the Younger home. Here, Walter Lee returns to the apartment with a contract he and his would-be business partners have put together, evidence for Lena that his plan is authentic and sensible according to Walter Lee. And yet, Lena has other concerns on her mind that evening, namely Ruth's pregnancy. Angered and disgusted by his mother's refusal to negotiate with him and consider the proposition, Walter Lee attempts to leave the apartment but is prevented by "Mama's" fierce and alarming command to sit down. In this pivotal scene, Walter Lee and his mother attempt to see each other eye to eye and articulate the transformations taking place within their household. The nucleus of the conflict centers on defining masculinity as both Walter Lee and his mother have disparate notions of what constitutes manhood and the function of the man. Regressing to his familiar role as a-mother's-son, Walter Lee, now on his knees, pleads with his seated mother:

> Mama, I want so many things that sometimes I think they're gonna drive me crazy. See, I'm thirty-five years old, and I ain't got nothing. I ain't gonna be nothing.... I open cars doors all day long. I drive a man around in his limousine and I say, "Yes, sir; no, sir; very good, sir; shall I take the Drive, sir?"... I don't know if I can make you understand.... Sometimes it's like I can see my future stretched out in front of me – just plain as day. The future, Mama. Hanging over there at the edge of my days...a big, looming blank space full of nothing.... But it don't have to be.... Sometimes when I'm downtown driving that man around, we pass them cool, quiet looking restaurants, and I look in. I see these white boys. They sit talking...about deals...worth millions of dollars and half the time they don't look no older than me. (*Raisin*)

Walter Lee's obsession with the insurance money stems from his desire to achieve a financial position separate from the one created and controlled by the matriarchal system in which he feels confined. His dreams of a better future and "becoming a man," however, translate as solipsistic in this scene when juxtaposed against Lena's interpretation of a man's role in the house.

Whereas Walter Lee maintains that his masculinity can be regained by financial success, and hence, his ability to control his life and stabilize his family under his personal supervision there in the traditional system of the city, Lena, as the only visible "'wheel of the family'" at this moment (qtd. in Keyser and Ruszkowski 60-61), views her son's entrepreneurial passions with disappointment and believes masculinity can only be defined by taking responsibility for the home and the crises which threaten to dismantle it. For her, abandoning the urban sphere for the suburban one is the only means for ensuring the security of her family. "You something new, boy," Lena says. "In my time, we was worried about not being lynched and getting to the North if we could and how to stay alive and still have a pinch of dignity too. Now here come you and Beneatha talking about 'bout things we ain't never even thought about hardly, me and your daddy. You ain't satisfied or proud of nothing we done. . . . You my children, but how different we done become" (*Raisin*). The epochal breach between Lena's generation and Walter Lee's clearly complicates an understanding of what constitutes privilege, opportunity, and rights, thus underscoring the popular Cold War notion that familial rebirth is only possible or permissible in the suburbs, an ideology Lena buys into.

Lena, grateful for no longer having to endure some of the vulgar and blatant acts of discrimination from whites, cannot understand why Walter Lee does not appreciate how she and her deceased husband suffered to reach a position where they did not have to ride at the back of the bus or be barred from voting. Walter Lee, however, harbors a volcanic rage against the overt and covert racism he experiences every day in his urban environment. To be grateful to have a few crumbs of freedom is unsuitable in Walter Lee's eyes, for he does not accept that he should remain in servitude to the white man. After all, he himself is a man, a man with dreams of wanting to make something of himself. "Here I am a giant," he complains, "surrounded by ants – ants who can't even understand what it is the giant is talking about" (*Raisin*). The fact that he is only permitted to listen to the conversations of white men, to speak when spoken to, is akin to a new kind of indentured service, a new kind of pain and anguish which the Cold War climate in the United States instituted to render his body obsolete and invisible. "'Every black man in America,'" according to black psychiatrists William Grier and Price Cobbs, "'has suffered such injury as to be realistically sad about the hurt done to him....He develops a sadness and intimacy with misery which has become a characteristic of black Americans. It is a cultural depression and a cultural masochism'" (qtd. in Segal 184) that burns at the center of Walter Lee's core. This is something he believes neither his mother, nor his wife, nor his sister are able to articulate: "You just don't understand, Mama," he says gravely, "you just don't understand" (*Raisin*).

Standing beside a mirror, Walter Lee delivers these lines and intensifies the symbolic icons that comprise the mise-en-scène. The mirror is there to reflect Walter Lee; however, we do not see his reflection in the shot. In *A Raisin in the Sun*, mirrors play a critical, yet subtle, role in both capturing and fragmenting images. If a reflection in the mirror represents an illusory identification with the self and the consequential severance from the mother figure in the Lacanian sense, then Walter Lee has not yet made this recognition and has not distinguished his identity from Lena's. As such, he has not yet come into being and has not reached the symbolic level of Lacan's mirror stage (Hayward 2). On the small dresser below the wall-mirror lays a picture of Walter Lee's son and one of his father; however, despite the film's attempt to align Walter Lee in this triangularity of masculine representation and lineage, he remains incomplete, a "fragmented body," according to Lacan (4), unable to recognize his otherness in the reflection, for he is still indistinguishable from the males in the photographs and from the women in the house.

The following scene equally captures this striking power-tension by challenging the constitution of masculinity that the earlier scene initiates. Lena, in an attempt to prevent Walter Lee from leaving the house in disgust over the last battle, informs him that Ruth is pregnant and is considering an abortion. Lena sits at an angle on her sofa chair in the frame's center, her authoritative space in the house and one from which she is depicted making crucial decisions for the family time and again. And yet, ironically, being placed in the filmic center conventionally constitutes disempowerment although her dialogue evokes a tone of control and dictation. Directly behind her is the mirror and dresser before which Walter Lee was standing, attempting to confirm his masculinity and autonomy. Walter, himself, is positioned in an extreme close-up shot in the right frame while Ruth emerges from the bedroom, her entire body visible in a long shot with arms in their customary folded position below her breasts, as though cold and invulnerable.

There at the family table, a traditional symbol of unity and discourse, Lena, with her grandson's and husband's photo bracketing her in the background, challenges her son to officiate this family crisis. The empty mirror behind her functions as a kind of absent-presence of the deceased father; it is a time-continuum, waiting to be filled by Walter. "Well son, I'm waiting to hear you say something," Lena, as familial-regent, pontificates from her chair. "I'm waiting to hear how you be your father's son. Be the man he was. Your wife says she going to destroy your child, and I'm waiting to hear you talk like him and say we a people who give children life, not who destroys them. I'm waiting to see you stand up and look like your daddy" (*Raisin*). As the shot ends with Lena rising up out of her chair and slapping the table as if to draw him out of a dreamscape, Walter Lee maintains his silence and abruptly leaves the apartment.

Walter Lee's inaction in this scene can thus be interpreted as his inability to come into his manhood, which is how Lena comprehends his behavior in this scene. "You are a disgrace to your father's memory," she derides (*Raisin*). In her eyes, Walter fails this opportunity to fill the empty space of the mirror and become the *paterfamilias*. And yet, the reconstruction of Walter Lee's masculinity is more complex than taking the reins of familial responsibility when upbraided by one's mother, for he refuses to accept that his manhood should be defined by someone else, someone who is not a man. Such a construction of a black masculinity is difficult to establish in that masculinity itself

> involves a certain level of personal autonomy and control over people and things. It is not some type of internal essence, which Black men have or lack, but the assumption and possession of an array of privileges many of which are denied most Black men. For the Black male underclass, like other men denied the usual confirmation of gender superiority, the only mechanisms of dominance available are frequently the mechanisms of self-destruction – internecine violence, sexual coercion and self-hatred. For Black men, however, there is the added poison of a cultural climate of devaluation, its literal racist contours now inscribed in language.... (Segal 187)

The masculine heterotopia of the black man differs in many respects from that of the white male; for the Cold War black man, emasculation emerges not only from suburban fetishes of liberty, but from wresting one's identity and power from white masculine supremacy. Nevertheless, drinking seems to be a temporary cure for Walter Lee's fractured masculinity. However, such masochistic endeavors do not cloud the reality that Walter Lee feels not only cheated, but denied an opportunity to function as a man on his own terms, under his own conditions, and in his own space.

A major turning point in *A Raisin in the Sun* is the scene in which Walter Lee is finally made head of the family by Lena. Significantly, it is also one of the few moments when the film digresses from the play's original script. In the film version, Lena finds Walter Lee drunk at his favorite bar. Deliberately out of place on multiple levels, Lena's figure is clothed in one of her old Sunday dresses and black flowery hats, and her displeasure in being in the hyper-masculine space of the bar is marked by her stern countenance. Swaying in his seat and slurring, having missed work for several days, Walter Lee tries to make eye contact with his mother. In a final bid to resurrect his entrepreneurial dream of financial autonomy, he attempts to parallel his desire for a world of opportunity and choices with his mother's exodus from the rural landscape of the South to the urban topography of the North, a journey many black families were making in the early decades of the twentieth century. Still, this dream is linked to drinking, for a liquor store can be seen as degrading rather than helping the black community, as is the case in Lena's perspective.

> WALTER LEE: Why did you leave the South? Forty years ago, when you were a young woman, why did you leave the South?
> LENA: I expect for the same reason everybody else does. I thought that maybe if I could come up here, I'd do better for myself. But I don't say I exactly turned over the world since then –
> WALTER LEE: But you didn't give nobody the right to stop you once you decided to go. Even though you weren't going no place at all, you thought you were, didn't you? Then why in the name of God couldn't you let me get on my train when my time come? I don't think it's ever gonna come again, Mama. (*Raisin*)

Whether Lena finally understands Walter Lee's misery through his opportunistic analogy or whether she can no longer bear watching her son sink into himself any longer, she hands over the remaining $6,500, having already placed a down payment on her suburban house in the all-white

Clybourne Park.

    She performs this act with the understanding that Walter Lee will set some of it aside for Beneatha's medical school expenses and take responsibility for the rest. "It ain't much," she says, "but it's all I got in the world, and I'm putting it in your hands. I'm telling you to be the head of this family from now on like you're supposed to be" (*Raisin*). From this gesture, the spectating audience is left to wonder if Walter Lee will ignore his mother's request and invest the money in his liquor store scheme or if he has finally come into his mother's definition of manhood and perceives her trust as a confirmation that she is now ready to transfer the familial power back to a patriarchal system. The scene that immediately follows reveals Walter Lee entering his and his wife's bedroom back at the apartment. As he approaches Ruth on the bed, his image is reflected in a wall-mirror, thus suggesting perhaps that Walter Lee has an identity different from his mother's, an identity which is contingent upon performing a responsible father/husband/son role. The brief scene closes with Walter Lee lying down on the bed and embracing Ruth, giving the audience the impression that "by conforming to the moralistic demands of the family unit" (Pines 106), he now has the ability to lead the family and is confirmed in his heteronormativity. *A Raisin in the Sun* continues moving centripetally towards a patriarchal system reminiscent of a Cold War domestic order in the American suburbs.

    While the power transference scene explicated above does take place in Hansberry's Broadway play version, it transpires in a different location and underscores Walter Lee's fantasies of living out the American Dream as an organization man. In the play version of the same scene, after Lena hands over the money to Walter Lee, he tells his son that he plans to complete the liquor store transaction and make all of them financially secure and stable. The idealized, almost television-like identity he creates for himself and the rest of his family is thus one that could come right out of an episode from one the many white suburban sitcoms popular at the time, such as *Donna Reed, Father Knows Best, Ozzie and Harriet*, or *Leave it to Beaver*.

> That's how come one day when you 'bout seventeen years old I'll come home and I'll be pretty tired...after a day of conferences and secretaries getting things wrong the way they do...'cause an executive's life is hell, man.... And I'll pull the car up on the driveway.... And I'll come up the steps to the house and the

gardener will be clipping away at the hedges.... And I'll go inside and Ruth will come downstairs and meet me at the door and we'll kiss each other and she'll take my arm and we'll go up to your room to see you sitting on the floor with the catalogues of all the great schools in America around you...and I hand you the world. (Hansberry 108-9)

The portrait of the Cold War nuclear family resonates in Walter Lee's image of a happy home, even if it is a world financed by an inner-city liquor store rather than by a gray flannel suit occupation. In this dream, his masculinity is confirmed and unchallenged by those around him, for such individuals who populate his dreamscape can only exist in relation to his omnipotence and benevolence. He will always have a place in this static and brave new world, and that place is at the center of power: the office secretaries will always need to be corrected, the gardener must always demonstrate respect for his altruistic employer, his TV-like wife will always greet him upon his return from the office, and his son will permanently be nearby to receive his father's charity. In his new locality, Walter Lee will no longer be the servant, but the one who is served. The money he has received from his mother opens up this new frontier of such possibilities and adds yet another image of masculinity to the heterotopia generated by suburbia. Walter Lee's father, reified through his death's monetary inheritance, has initiated the cycle of endowment, and this title of endowment must now be passed on to his son with the expectation that the legacy will continue on to Travis, thus securing the Younger males' participation in the American Dream, and thereby guaranteeing the cycle of patriarchy. Inheritance and entitlement manifest themselves via suburban homeownership during the Cold War, for this "constitutes the single greatest source of wealth for white Americans" (32), according to George Lipsitz:

[Suburban homeownership] is the factor most responsible for the disparity between blacks and whites in respect to wealth – a disparity between the two groups much greater than their differences in income. It is the basis for intergenerational transfers of wealth that enable white parents to give their children financial advantages over the children of other groups. Housing plays a crucial role in determining educational opportunities as well, because school funding based on property tax assessments in most localities gives better opportunities to white children than to children from minority communities. (32-33)

Suburbia, then, becomes the only viable means through which a man can attain success and happiness in the Cold War, and Walter Lee seems willing now to enter a world to which he believes he is entitled despite the reality that such a world still rejects him. Although the film's and play's version of the transference of power unfolds in different sites (a bar and the apartment, respectively), the importance of forging the spatial anatomy of masculine domination creates a parallel between the depictions. Whereas the bar clearly demonstrates a field of phallocentricity, the private dialogue between father and son establishes a discursive space within an anticipated suburban realm for patriarchal lineage.

The exuberance Walter Lee feels after completing his business transaction is evident in the film version scene that follows the one at the bar. Absent from the original play, the visitation to the new suburban home underscores the disparity that exists between the waning world of the black urban ghetto and the sanitized sphere of white suburbia. Dressed in their Sunday best, the Younger family members inspect their new residence. Bathed in light, spacious and clean, the house in Clybourne Park provides a stage upon which each of the characters may recreate their identities and positions in the family. Unlike the medium close-ups that framed the Youngers claustrophobically in their Southside apartment, the camera uses medium long shots to epitomize the spatial expanse of the home. While Ruth and Lena open cabinets and drawers, Beneatha seems almost to float down the hall, taking a mental count of the many bedrooms. A sunlit image of a window reflects against the end of the hall, perhaps reminiscent of the only window each of them shared in the apartment. While Walter Lee glides about the floor space and affectionately touches his family members, the happiness and satisfaction he feels as suburban *paterfamilias* is evident. Clearly, the film reinforces the utopic space suburbia created in popular thought during the Cold War: a space ruled by pleasure, security, normalcy – and domesticated masculinity.

According to the ideal fostered during the early years of the Cold War, living in the suburbs was thought to amalgamate home and family within the refuge of a homogenous community. This notion was unabashedly reinforced by the proliferation of television situation comedies throughout the 1950s and 1960s which "helped to facilitate the psychic as well as the physical mass migration to the suburbs" (Beuka 72).

However, much of what has been conceptualized as suburban, and most of what is theorized or depicted as the utopic ideal of suburbia comes from the mythologizing of this non-urban landscape, for the reality of suburbia has been constructed by a manufactured image of mythical suburbia, and in turn, this image of suburbia has become, in many ways, the American reality.

For many middle-class white American families in the Cold War, the ownership of single-family homes in the suburbs, away from the perceived suffocation of the urban-scape was quite attractive. For the Younger family, owning a home of their own will afford them the opportunity for a better life and a chance to disappear culturally behind the veil of white society. *A Raisin in the Sun* sells the idea to both white and black audiences that this new social and economic geography has become the American Dream reborn, a matrix of lifestyle and expression, the contemporary Manifest Destiny, a new occasion to redefine and redesign the American landscape. However, depicting a black family breaching this racial acropolis does not celebrate a kind of new pluralism thought to be emerging in the United States during the Cold War; rather, *A Raisin in the Sun* normalizes the mythology that the American Dream exists and can be an equalizer for all families. While it was true that black families were moving out to the suburbs during the Cold War, their numbers were few and far between, for there was "no significant desegregation of the suburbs [taking] place" (Lipsitz 7).[2] Despite the fact that people insist on living out their utopic fantasies in the environs of suburbia, "they fail to recognize that they create and live in heterotopia" (Morales 23). The multiple forms of masculinities Walter Lee confronts throughout *Raisin*, that of the urban entrepreneur, the black man, the servant, the organization man, or the suburban *paterfamilias*, collide with one another and prove that suburbia is generating a kaleidoscope of roles and images. More importantly, this further debunks the argument that there remains a singular, ideal construction of the postwar American male.

The realities of racism in the Cold War suburb surface when a representative of the Clybourne Park Improvement Association pays a visit to the Youngers' apartment in Southside. In an attempt to bribe the Youngers not to occupy the Clybourne Park house, Karl Lindner (John Fiedler) informs Walter Lee, Ruth, and Beneatha through polite smiles and acts of gentility that their family is not welcome, for their presence in the white suburban community would potentially undermine the homogenous system the homeowners worked hard to construct.

> But you've got to admit that a man, right or wrong, has the right to want to have the neighborhood he lives in a certain kind of way. And at the moment the overwhelming majority of our people out there feel that people get along better, take more of a common interest in the life of the community, when they share a common background. I want you to believe me when I tell you that race prejudice simply doesn't enter into it. It is a matter of the people of Clybourne Park believing, rightly or wrongly, as I say, that for the happiness of all concerned that our Negro families are happier when they live in their own communities…. People can get awful worked up when they feel that their whole way of life and everything they've worked for is threatened. (*Raisin*)

This display of bigotry is off-putting to the characters, but they somehow do not seem completely surprised by this racist reception. After all, white suburbanites belong to a position of power and privilege they have inherited through a very controlled history of discrimination and supremacy. Containing black families behind the Cold War urban curtain of poverty and subjugation permits white Americans to live in a *sanitized* environment, free from social and ethnic *contamination*. Karl Lindner, the arbiter of this ethnic force, is only there to re-inform them of their social station. To make matters worse, Walter Lee's business deal fails as he is swindled by one of his partners. The inheritance money entrusted to him has been lost. He is thus relegated, once again, to the role of the *castrated son*. In these two scenes, Walter Lee is reminded of who he is: a poor, powerless black man, rendered invisible by the white supremacy of the dominant class. Wailing at the feet of his weeping mother, who cannot believe her son has placed the family in such jeopardy, he can only passively endure the verbal blows of his mother's chastising requiem:

> I seen him [Walter Lee's father]…night after night…come in and look at that rug, and then look at me, the red showing in his eyes, the veins moving in his head. I seen him grow thin and old before he was forty, working and working and working like somebody's old horse, killing himself. And you – you give it all away in a day. (*Raisin*)

In an effort to evade further tragedy and spare his family members any more misery, Walter Lee decides to rectify the situation by surrendering to the racist alienation of the Clybourne Park suburb and to accept Mr. Lindner's offer to have his committee buy the house from the Youngers. Violating the historical pride of his family of "five generations of people who was slaves and sharecroppers" (*Raisin*), Walter Lee struggles to salvage his masculinity and power over the family.

> What's the matter with you all! I didn't make this world. It was give to me this way. Yes, I want me some yachts someday. Yes, I want to hang some real pearls 'round my wife's neck. Ain't she supposed to wear no pearls? Somebody tell me, tell me who decides which women is suppose to wear pearls in this world. I tell you I am a man, and I think my wife should wear some pearls in this world. (*Raisin*)

Walter Lee's maxim that "money is life" is rearticulated here in this scene. Believing that opportunities come to the urban black male in disfigured forms and contours, Walter Lee will take the white man's financial compensation and accept the servile position as a second class citizen in order to duplicate financial "success." No longer permitted to become the entrepreneur of the city nor the organization man of the suburb, his dreams of personal advancement and masculine self-recognition have been splintered and confined to spaces found undesirable by the white middle-class. Such a domestic policy of social and economic alienation typifies the racial othering transpiring in the Cold War United States and contributes to a larger, more invisible containment narrative as revealed in this film. "That's your [the white man's] neighborhood out there," he speaks rhetorically before his family, anticipating what he will say during Lindner's return. "You got the right to keep it like you want. Just write the check and the house is yours" (*Raisin*). A disappointment to his family, Walter Lee relegates his identity to a mere shadow in the blinding light of white masculine domination. Walter Lee, in failing at his own attempt to wrest an identity of urban success and liberation, is now just a hollow shell of man, for "[t]here is nothing left to love," according to his younger sister Beneatha. In Walter Lee's disintegrating world, the touchstone of success is sharing in the prosperity of his white male counterparts. Because he is less concerned about questioning or dismantling the socio-economic locales that are actually keeping him down, Walter Lee also fails to recognize the discriminatory practices inherent in the American system of capitalism.

The climactic scene in *A Raisin in the Sun* becomes Walter Lee's final testing site for his manhood and familial authority. In accepting Mr. Lindner's bid to buy out the rights of the Clybourne property, he realizes that he would be forcing his family further down in their shame and disenfranchisement. In the play and film's closing scene, when Mr. Lindner returns under the assumption that the Youngers have accepted his offer, he is met with coldness and disdain by the Younger women. Positioned in different spaces of the living room area, the women avert their eyes from Lindner's gaze and anticipate Walter Lee's abdicating monologue; Travis, his son, is the only member of the family whose face remains firmly fixed on Walter Lee's. Like a testimony of faith, Walter Lee stands unabashedly before Lindner, and in a turn of events, retraces his paternal lineage as a confirmation that he is aware of the ancestry that the dominant culture has historically sought to erase. He is now unwilling to sacrifice what his father has made possible, what his father "earned for [them] brick by brick" (*Raisin*).

In this grand gesture of power and potency, Walter Lee is finally able to recognize simultaneously who he is as a man, a son, a brother, a husband, and a father. This is the legacy that constitutes Walter Lee's masculinity and empowerment, for he must embody the spirit of suburban patriarchy and abandon the waning apparition of frontierism and entrepreneurship associated with the city, that is, if he is to succeed in migrating his family from the spaces of urbanity to the domestic sphere of Clybourne Park. "We come from people who had a lot of pride...we are very proud people," he insists to an astonished Lindner (*Raisin*). As Travis quietly utters something to his father, Walter Lee embraces him, pulling his head towards his belly as if protecting him from Mr. Lindner, and thus underscoring his control over the space of the scene and those within it. "This is my son," he declares proudly, "and he makes the sixth generation. The sixth generation of my family in this country" (*Raisin*). Although not knowing who you are can be a universal crisis, the anxiety and crisis the Cold War develops for the middle-class white male does not generate the same socio-political tension as it has for Walter Lee. In *Nobody Knows My Name*, James Baldwin addresses this issue:

> I thought that the white world was very different from the world I was moving out of and I turned out to be entirely wrong. It seemed different. It seemed safer, at least the white people

seemed safer. It seemed cleaner, it seemed more polite, and, of course, it seemed much richer from the material point of view. But I didn't meet anyone in that world who didn't suffer from the very same affliction that all the people I had fled from suffered from and that was that they didn't know who they were. They wanted to be something that they were not.... I had stepped into, I had walked right into...the bottomless confusion which is both public and private, of the American republic. (148-49)

In this sense, the essence of Walter Lee's crisis of alienation and marginalization, that is the crisis that his masculine heterotopia generates, stems from the denial of his personage and his very history of subjugation by white privilege. As such, it is important to recognize that "[a] people deprived of political sovereignty finds it very nearly impossible to recreate, for itself, the image of its past, this perpetual recreation being an absolute necessity for, if not, indeed, the definition of a living culture" (Baldwin 15). Equally important, it proves the invisibility of marginalized groups, such as the black community, by containing them behind the white plight of rhetoric and identity anxieties of the organization man.

However, shifting from a culture of crisis to one of vitality is a central message in *A Raisin in the Sun* and further illustrates Hansberry's desire to convey "that black pride was a new reality on the American scene" (Keyser and Ruszkowski 63). The richness and vitality of Hansberry's drama is further significant in articulating black identity and consciousness at the start of the 1960s because it initiated the discourse of black entitlement and institutionalized disenfranchisement in the everyday experience of African Americans. And yet, ironically at the center of this socio-psychological liberation among African Americans, it was the black male who was granted dominion over the black female as a means for articulating and recovering his masculinity.

In a vain attempt to solicit the intervention of Lena, Mr. Lindner defers to the old matriarch of the family, hoping that she will be more reasonable than her son. Avoiding his gaze, and with tears slowly running down her cheeks, Lena proudly relinquishes her authority to her son: "I'm afraid you don't understand. My son said we was gonna move, and there ain't nothing left for me to say" (*Raisin*). She is seated in her chair, the chair that has come to symbolize her authority in the family, and is reflected in the multiple mirrors of the cabinet beside her. The absent-presence of the deceased father the mirror signified earlier in the film has now been filled by Walter Lee. No longer viable as the family's authoritative buttress, Lena has become the fragmented body in the mirrors, thus symbolizing a restoration of power to the patriarchy. If the city has come to represent a feminine space in this film, a space comprised of close-knit contacts, of a matriarchy that inhibits the male from coming into his full manhood, then the suburb epitomizes the historical shift to a masculine space, one of autonomy and of patriarchal control over the nuclear family.

On the surface, *A Raisin in the Sun* melodramatically suggests to a white audience that black American families have dreams of upward mobility and suffer from a legacy of a social and economic disavowal from the dominant class. And yet, the film reinforces the myth that suburbia is a site where tragedies end, lives are reborn, and men are empowered by dignity and autonomy. For even Walter Lee wants Lindner to deliver the message, "We don't want to make no trouble for nobody or fight no causes, and [that] we'll try to be good neighbors," neighbors who are safe and will easily assimilate into the white ideal of the suburban topography. In so doing, we can posit that the Youngers are moving from one discriminating place to another, from the subjugating system of the city, to the alienating apparatus of the suburbs.

Equally neglected by the film is the new role of the women in the Younger family. After Lindner leaves the apartment, having failed to secure his proposition, the family returns to their playful bantering characteristic of the first half of the film – but with added benevolence and a new deferment to Walter Lee's authority. Beneatha proudly announces a marriage proposal from a Nigerian intellectual who has been pursing her throughout the duration of the film. However, Walter Lee, in his role as patriarch of the new spatial order, scolds her for thinking that she will make this decision on her own:

> WALTER LEE: Girl, you better get them silly notions out of your Head once and for all and start looking for a man with some loot.
> BENEATHA: Now what do you have to do with who I marry?
> WALTER LEE: Plenty. I'm head of this family.

While the exchange is meant to be playful (in fact, Lena is depicted in the frame shaking her head and smiling approvingly at what she hears), it italicizes the subjugation that the women will experience living in the suburbs, and it marks their bodies within the restrictive parameters of masculine domination. If "[c]ontainment was the key to [suburban] security" during the Cold War (May 13), then the sustaining of the suburban patriarchy was contingent upon relegating women behind the Brocade Curtain of domesticity. The fact that Walter Lee has squandered the inheritance is lost upon the audience by the play/film's end. A portion of that money was to be invested in Beneatha's medical education. However, this will no longer transpire under Walter Lee's governance. The best she can hope for is to remain *beneath* (a play on her own name) the authority of masculine domination and quit her pontification of African American women's rights. Indeed, Walter Lee has "come into his manhood," albeit a suburban one, according to Lena, "kind of like the rainbow after the rain" (*Raisin*). However, this transformation, a seemingly natural and inevitable one through its filmic rendering, reinstitutes the social construction that the Cold War suburb is a site of harmony and liberty for all who inhabit this spatial envelope.

The American Dream expresses the individual's aspirations and desires, those typified by personal gain and solitary achievement. From the very beginning of *A Raisin in the Sun*, Walter Lee embodies this solipsistic drive to better himself first and his family second, if entirely at all. "I'm trying to talk to you about me!" Walter Lee insists while Ruth serves him his eggs in the film's opening scene (*Raisin*). "Here, the reference 'me' does not include the promise of medical education for his sister Beneatha," according to Mark A. Reid, "nor does it include placing a down payment on a new home for the Younger family. Walter's desire does not encompass a group consciousness, and his entrepreneurial desire ignores the collective dreams that sustain the Younger family" (63-64). This American Dream is brought to fruition by placing the needs and wants of the patriarch before the basic rights of women, an explosive issue during the Cold War. And yet, rather than "[mirroring] the black woman's growing awareness of her right to reject motherhood and plan parenthood around her professional career" (66), Reid, like other critics, asserts that the film relapses into the conventional roles of dominating male and subjugated female. Ruth will be designated to the role of motherhood once again; Beneatha will marry "a man with some loot" and one of whom Walter approves. Eventually, Lena will slowly fade in her function as extended family member. It will only be Travis, Walter Lee's progeny, who will inherit his father's patriarchal power, and thus, define his own masculinity by modeling his father's suburban identity.

A Raisin in the Sun promises that conflicts and their subsequent resolutions are made possible through an abandonment of the urban spaces and an exodus to patriarchal suburban ones. More importantly, it means that urban space will decay, that dreams will never be realized in the city, and that happiness will only come from capitulating to patriarchy and other masculine structures. Thus, by recycling the mythos that suburbia is the realization of the American Dream in which upward mobility is the unifying catalyst in familial stability, *A Raisin in the Sun* underscores the Cold War system that sought in its efforts to redesign the anatomy of the dominant class and insure its supremacy for the remaining half of the twentieth century.

Notes

1. This notion of domestic desire and eating of eggs as expressed by Ruth was taken from Dr. Amy Ongiri's October 9, 2002, lecture on the play/film in her ENG 138T course at University of California, Riverside. For this idea, I wish to thank Dr. Ongiri.
2. "From 1960 to 1977, 4 million whites moved out of central cities, while the number of whites living in suburbs increased by 22 million; during the same years, the inner-city black population grew by 6 million, but the number of blacks living in suburbs increased by only 500,000" (Lipsitz 7). Once white suburban dwellers' lives commenced, they soon came to realize that there was a price for living within an idyllic terrain. That price was exacted by marginalizing groups who did not model white familial constructions, abandoning urban centers to decay and ruin, and tearing up the land for wires, roads, sewers, and shopping centers.

Works Cited

Baldwin, James. *Nobody Knows My Name: More Notes of a Native Son*. New York: Vintage Books, 1993.

Beuka, Robert. *SuburbiaNation: Reading Suburban Landscape in Twentieth-Century American Fiction and Film*. New York: Palgrave, 2004.

Bogle, Donald. *Toms, Coons, Mulattoes, Mammies, and Bucks: An Interpretive History of Blacks in American Films*, 3rd ed. New York: Continuum, 1998.

Corber, Robert J. *Homosexuality in Cold War America: Resistance and the Crisis of Masculinity*. Durham and London: Duke UP, 1997.

Hansberry, Lorraine. *A Raisin in the Sun*. New York: Vintage Books, 1958, 1994.

Hayward, Susan. *Key Concepts in Cinema Studies*. London and New York: Routledge, 1996.

Jackson, Kenneth T. *Crabgrass Frontier: The Suburbanization of the United States*. New York and Oxford: Oxford UP, 1985.

Keyser, Lester J., and André H. Ruszkowski. *The Black Man's Changing Role on the American Screen: The Cinema of Sidney Poitier*. San Diego and New York: A.S. Barnes & Company, Inc., 1980.

Lacan, Jacques. *Erits: A Selection*. Trans. Alan Sheridan. New York: W.W. Norton & Company, Inc., 1977.

Lipsitz, George. *The Possessive Investment in Whiteness: How White People Profit from Identity Politics*. Philadelphia: Temple UP, 1998.

Marill, Alvin H. *The Films of Sidney Poitier*. Secaucus, NJ: The Citadel Press, 1978.

May, Elaine Tyler. *Homeward Bound: American Families in the Cold War Era*. New York: Basic Books, 1988.

Morales, Alejandro. "Dynamic Identities in Heterotopia." *Alejandro Morales: Fiction Past, Present, Future Perfect*. Ed. Jose Antonio Gurpegui. Tempe, AZ: Bilingual Review/Press, 1996. 14-27.

Mulvey, Laura. "Visual Pleasure and Narrative Cinema." *The Sexual Subject: A Screen Reader in Sexuality*. London and New York: Routledge, 1992: 22-34.

Pines, Jim. *Blacks in Films: A Survey of Racial Themes and Images in the American Film*. London: Studio Vista, Cassell & Collier Macmillan Publishers Limited, 1975.

A Raisin in the Sun. Dir. Daniel Petrie. 1961. DVD. Columbia Pictures, 1989.

Reid, Mark A. *Redefining Black Film*. Berkeley, Los Angeles, Oxford: U of California P, 1993.

Rotella, Carlo. *October Cities: The Redevelopment of Urban Literature*. Berkeley and Los Angeles: U of California P, 1998

Segal, Lynne. *Slow Motion: Changing Masculinities, Changing Men*. New Brunswick, NJ: Rutgers UP, 1990

110

6

Policing Traumatized Boundaries of Self and Nation:
Undocumented Labor in *Blade Runner*

Anil Narine

Fear, revulsion, and horror were the emotions which the
big-city crowd aroused in those who first observed it.
-Walter Benjamin, *Illuminations*

I. Introduction

When Ridley Scott's *Blade Runner* was released in 1982, American, and
especially Californian, industry was in the midst of a recession that
affected nearly every industrialized nation. Following the 1979 jump in oil
prices, the second major increase in five years, industrial production
around the globe dropped between 5 and 10 percent, a trajectory that did
not cease until 1983 (Veenhoven and Hagenaars 2). Since the early 1970s,
American industries, especially the manufacturing sector, had been relying
upon methods of "flexible accumulation" that allowed them to compete
globally by repealing some of American workers' rights and unionized
power, and by exploiting budding labor markets in Southeast Asia and
Mexico. In the decade following the prosperous 1960s, America's global
position as the lone, victorious economic powerhouse, along with the
middle class livelihoods its economy supported, were challenged, and both
the American working and middle classes felt the threat. Japan and
Germany, whose economies were strong by the late sixties, had forced
American "corporations into a period of rationalization, restructuring, and
intensification of labor control" in an effort to lower production costs
(Harvey 145). This restructuring of traditional labor processes angered
workers, especially those whose jobs had been relocated or made
contractual, in keeping with the need for a flexible labor force. Although

workers on the factory floor or in the service industries were the most immediately affected, these changes also weighed heavily on the minds of middle class managers, who became acutely aware of workers' grievances as the 1980-82 recession wore on and increasingly apprehensive about the possibility of vengeful workers rising up. Thus, in California, members of the working class felt threatened by new, cheaper labor forces and lost many of their hard-won rights, along with the sense of security these maintained. Members of the American middle class, however, were far from immune; as they bore witness to the unenviable plight of their blue-collar counterparts, they also feared joining them – a "fear of falling," as Barbara Ehrenreich phrased it – from their positions of precarious privilege that *Blade Runner* both registers and, problematically, elicits. This fear is intensified by an arguably racist *mise-en-scène* that depicts Los Angeles in the year 2019 as an urban wasteland overrun by largely squalid, multicultural masses who represent, along with the humanoid invaders, the new face of California's working class. These crowds, I suggest, invoke "fear" and "revulsion" in viewers because they seem poised to engulf our white, middle class protagonist, Rick Deckard (Harrison Ford), who himself fears joining these "little people" (Fancher 4).

Based loosely on Philip K. Dick's novel *Do Androids Dream of Electric Sheep?* (1969), *Blade Runner* is also a reworking of Mary Shelley's *Frankenstein* (1818) and other incarnations of the Prometheus myth, which dramatizes the insurrection and revenge of fabricated humanoid laborers who are exploited and then abandoned by their capitalist creators. The horror and suspense of the film rely on the threat posed by four such "replicants" who vanquish their unlucky bosses in an off-world, forced-labor, mining colony and survive the journey back to Los Angeles (as opposed to the novel's San Francisco setting). There, they want only to confront their creators, to lodge a grievance over the unfair conditions in which they must live and work, and to find out how to lengthen their four-year lifespans. The replicants represent colonial slaves in the world of the film, which is replete with references to colonies, mutinies, and "skin jobs," a term for the replicants which Deckard's voiceover equates with the racial slur "nigger," found only in history books. And yet, as invaders whose very presence in California is illegal, the incoming replicants can also be read as undocumented immigrant workers whose ambitions are linked uneasily with those of the mysterious Mexican detective, Gaff (Edward James Olmos), who exhibits sympathies for the replicants even though he is gunning for Deckard's job killing them. Although *Blade Runner* has been widely read as a postmodernist pastiche of film noir and science fiction genres that questions the distinction between "human and non-human (artificial) intelligence" (Tasker 225), a major element of the narrative has received less scrutiny: namely, the way the colonial subplot allegorizes middle class anxieties about vengeful workers rising up and demanding answers from their superiors, and working class fears about being replaced by ambitious immigrants, whose invasion the borders and "security fences" (as they are called in the film) can no longer prevent.

II. Surveillance and the Optics of Power

The chief method of border patrol deployed in the film to combat the invading replicant workers is telling since it takes the form of visual scrutiny. Given that Los Angeles, as it is depicted, is home to every conceivable ethnic group, and numerous artificial life forms, the replicant invaders – all Caucasian – blend right in. An elaborate method of scrutiny is thus required to locate them amid the crowds. The Voight Kampff test, which determines the presence or absence of the subject's humanity by examining the fluctuation of its retina when certain emotions are elicited, serves this function in the film, which opens with a scene in which the test is administered. The device is clearly represented as a futuristic relative of much older methods of scrutiny, such as photography, which came to "play a central and complicitous role in…the articulation of race and racial differences" in nineteenth-century, colonial anthropology (Green 31). Like colonial photography, which was used to demonstrate anatomical inferiority, criminality, and barbarity, the Voight Kampff test establishes "a normalising gaze, a surveillance that makes it possible to qualify, to classify and to punish" (Foucault 25). The gaze of the Blade Runner detectives in the film initially functions in this way, since their techniques of observation are a means of distinguishing, judging, and ultimately condemning the undocumented invaders.

Eyes are one of the most prominent images in *Blade Runner*. The film opens with a skyline shot of a polluted Los Angeles at dusk, but quickly, the screenplay tells us, the "camera moves into a window in the large pyramid-shaped building. A man is sitting at a table. Another man enters the room and sits down. The following scene is reflected in the eye until Holden is seated. The eye is magnified and deeply revealed…. The eye is brown in a tiny screen. On a metallic screen below, the words

Voight Kampff are finely etched" (Fancher 1). Holden (Morgan Paull) is a Blade Runner. The eye in which he is reflected belongs to Leon (Brion James), who may be a replicant. Setting the tone for the various modes of detection and surveillance that follow, the film thus opens with the administration of a computerized eye exam. It is one of many ironies in the film that humans must rely on machines to assess the danger posed by machines; and people even use machines to assess their own humanity. The Voight Kampff machine nonetheless itemizes anatomical differences with a high degree of certainty and if the subject is deemed deviant and inhuman, it is executed, or forcefully "retired" to use the euphemism of the future.

Surveillance and differentiation are instrumental in policing the porous borders of selfhood. According to Rey Chow, "visuality determines the nature of the social object" to the extent that "the production of the West's 'others' depends on a logic of visuality that bifurcates 'subjects' and 'objects' into the incompatible positions of intellectuality and spectacularity" (60). Chow's subjects, like Green's colonial anthropologists and *Blade Runner's* detectives, are thinkers, the possessors and wielders of knowledge whose gaze is active and operative. The objects of the gaze, according to the power structures to which Chow refers, must only have knowledge produced about them, all the better to control them. They function best as objects if they are seen but not heard from. That is, they are their bodies, designed in *Blade Runner* for mining, military, and "pleasure" services. As the Blade Runner, Holden, administers the test, he feels confident in his superior knowledge; the gauges, meters, and dials on his Voight Kampff machine will ostensibly tell him all he needs to know about the seemingly nervous Leon, whose retina is grotesquely magnified on the machine's monitor. The detective begins his inquiry:

> [Holden smiles a patronizing smile.]…
> HOLDEN: You're in a desert, walking along…when…you look down and see a tortoise. It's crawling toward you…
> LEON: A tortoise. What's that?
> HOLDEN: Know what a turtle is?
> LEON: Of course.
> HOLDEN: Same thing.
> LEON: I never seen a turtle.
> [He sees Holden's patience is wearing thin.]
> LEON: But I understand what you mean. (Fancher 3)

Holden and Leon, the upholder and the violator of the law, appear to be playing out a traditional scene of interrogation, which affirms the subject's knowledge and the object's naiveté, in this case about the natural world. But the power relationship is not what it seems; in fact, it is a charade that embodies a disturbing process of identification. That is, the threatening notion that the policeman may have misidentified his suspect – that he may have identified with him as another human – looms uneasily beneath the apparent banality of the words exchanged. Leon, who has cleverly infiltrated the Tyrell Corporation that created him by posing as a janitor (aligning him with the working class) is far from naive. Rather, he is playing a cruel game with his interrogator, stalling Holden's efforts to discover what he inevitably will. Holden's sense of patronizing control over those he is employed to identify and segregate is, then, also false. When "the needles in the computer barely move," Holden knows he has identified an inhuman life form (Fancher 4). But by the time he reaches for his gun, "Leon is faster," shooting him repeatedly in a shocking display of speed (Fancher 4). Holden has failed in his inferences, or perhaps, ironically, because of his all too human reaction time. Although he had been studying the movements of the malicious "object" of his gaze, that object had been returning his gaze – and perhaps with more skill and sharper reflexes.

III. Trauma as a Narrative Stimulus

In a film about policing the permeable, traumatized boundaries between selves and others, Americans and replicant-invaders, it is significant that the plot should begin with such a violent act. Practically speaking, violence not only constitutes the action in the "action film," it stimulates further action and therefore drives narrative trajectories like the one Deckard follows as a salaried killer. Ridley Scott is unusually skilled at mobilizing this strategy, as evidenced by the opening swordfight in *The Duellists* (1977), the eruption of a creature from a man's stomach during a meal that motivates the action in *Alien* (1979), the stabbings carried out by Yakuza hit men in the opening restaurant scene of *Black Rain* (1989), the sexual assault and revenge killing outside the roadhouse that motivates the action in *Thelma and Louise* (1991; see Russell), the murder of Marcus Aurelius that initiates the hero's journey in *Gladiator* (2000), and the warlord shootings, interrupting the distribution of food in Somalia, that violently begin his *Blackhawk Down* (2001). The violence in *Blade Runner*, however, also plays a more thematic role. It agitates previously stable (however meticulously constructed) notions of selfhood. Notably, violence inspires various characters in the film, especially Rachael (Sean Young), Deckard, and his nemesis Roy (Rutger Hauer), to re-examine the violent or complicit roles they play in the larger late-capitalist economy for which they have sacrificed so much, including the protagonist's marriage and his emotions: "Replicants weren't supposed to have feelings, neither were Blade Runners," Deckard says in his voiceover. That is, as Judith Herman suggests,

> Traumatic events call into question basic human relationships. They breach the attachments of family, friendship, love and community. They shatter the construction of the self that is formed and sustained in relation to others.... They violate the victim's faith in a natural or divine order and cast the victim into a state of existential crisis. (51)

Family and friendship have no place in the film, except in fabricated childhood photographs like the ones Rachael discovers are fraudulent depictions of a childhood that was never hers; love, too, is a complicated endeavour because Deckard falls in love with Rachael, one of the machines he was employed to kill.

Selfhood, the identification of the other, and the methods of literal and metaphorical border patrol that police these categories become the central focus of the narrative even more than the film noir mystery. This shift results in human and non-human existential dilemmas: Deckard had been "an ex-cop, an ex-Blade Runner" and a "cold fish" to his "ex-wife." In our first encounter with him, as the camera marauds through an outdoor food court, he is difficult to distinguish from the masses of people who surround him. As he comes into focus, we see that he is, tellingly, scanning the Help Wanted ads for his next role, leaving us to ponder, who is he now? Interestingly, Giuliana Bruno links the replicants with schizophrenia, a psychological condition she defines as "the inability to experience the persistence of the 'I' over time" resulting in a "perpetual present" (189). Deckard, it seems, suffers from this condition at least as severely as those he polices. He is ex-everything and soon-to-be-nothing. He lives, like the late-capitalist landscape he inhabits, with "no conceivable future on the horizon" (Jameson 119). Does he have a place in society when he is not a fierce oppressor of the illegitimate, undocumented workforce – the "little people" he threatens, in one scene, with liquor violation fines, and the replicants he threatens with death? What will be his function if the replicant workers achieve equal opportunity status? What would be the result of his identification with them as equals? After all, their fears of mortality, their immobility, their suffering, and their existential questions are the same as his own. Does Deckard enact power, given that he is an extension of the state, or is he, himself, a slave to his utilitarian function within the repressive apparatus? In short, who is he without his other?

IV. Fears of Falling

Such questions haunt those in middle class professions who fear being subsumed by the underclass and who begin questioning the extent to which they themselves differ from the "little people." Just as the Freudian infant, whose cry summons its mother, feels both omnipotent when she arrives with the breast or the blanket and fearful about losing its potency if one day she does not, Deckard oscillates between these conflicting sensations of supremacy and insecurity. Even though patrolling the border between those in power and those who service them is the central activity performed by the authority figures in the film, still the distinction breaks down and the borders become permeable. Deckard, one such figure of authority, is always also a servant to the power structure he represents, as we see when he submits to Police Chief Bryant's (M. Emmet Walsh) request that he return from retirement to hunt down Leon and the other escaped replicants:

> BRYANT: …This is a bad one, the worst yet. I need the old Blade
> Runner. I need your magic….
> DECKARD: I was quit when I walked in here [pause]. I'm twice
> as quit now. See ya, Bryant…
> BRYANT: Stop…right where you are!
> [Deckard freezes at the hard tone.]
> BRYANT: You know the score pal. When you're not a cop,
> you're little people.
> DECKARD: Forgot there for a minute about the little people. No
> choice, I guess.
> BRYANT: No choice, pal. (Fancher 4)

If the replicants have no choice about the length of their four-year lives, Deckard has no choice about the quality of his. He obviously despises his job as a killer, and yet it keeps him off the street and ninety-seven floors above it in his lonely studio, where liquor is his pacifier.[1] His power in his society, as a white male representing the law, is also a type of powerlessness because, like the underclass, he has so few options. We begin to wonder just how distinct he is from the poor masses over which he ostensibly wields authority. Furthermore, since he clearly gives in to his captain's rhetoric in the scene quoted above, we might also wonder to whom (or to what forces) Deckard is really submitting. Kevin McNamara finds it odd that the film never "open[s] onto the political power structure above Captain Bryant" (430). He suggests that "the omission of politics from the film's world [is] indicative of the postmodernization of power" because "there exists no identifiable source" (430). Instead, "power circulates through sophisticated management systems that are so internationalised, so technical that they are beyond the control of any person or cartel" (431). Like the androids in its service, society under capital has, itself, become a machine. It operates without human agency, it seems, and yet it prescribes, with little flexibility, the roles humans must play within it. Bryant's identification of a jobless Deckard with the masses of "little people" thus shocks him into submission: it stops Deckard in his tracks, eliciting angst and fear that he may lose the few "privileges of whiteness" he enjoys, and that he may become economically indistinguishable from the poor masses of Mexicans, Asians, Hare Krishnas, Arabs, and Skin Jobs he polices (431).

It is significant that Deckard is followed throughout the action by a mysterious character named Gaff (Olmos), whom the 1981 screenplay also names "the Mexican." Gaff has an inexplicable ability to locate Deckard anywhere in the city, and he seems intent on antagonizing Deckard throughout his unpleasant mission. Like Deckard, we begin to have the nagging suspicion that, should he refuse to work amid these conditions, "his job would fall to [his] non-white subordinate, Gaff, and his social privilege would be revoked" (McNamara 431). Thus, Deckard, too, is a slave: a victim, however, of his class privileges, or rather, of his obligation to continue playing the role defined for him in society under capital, despite the fact that he has had "a belly full of killing" which has left him traumatized. Indeed, as Bryant tells him, he has no choice: if the replicants threaten American lives, the Mexicans threaten their jobs.

In this sense, then, the violent Leon and the other replicants are only the most recent menacing immigrants to arrive from foreign lands in Scott's dystopian fantasy. Leon, Roy, Pris (Darryl Hannah), and Zhora (Joanna Cassidy) pose a literal threat to human safety through their vengeful quest for equal rights, but Gaff and the numerous other immigrant faces that populate the crowded sidewalks are also intended to appear threatening, at least to Californian livelihoods. Los Angeles is traumatized, then, from without and from within. It is the "Third World inside the first" (Bruno 186); those who once labored in Asia, the Subcontinent, and Latin America producing America's electronics, food, and clothes are no longer peripheral and invisible, but now inhabit the city. For these reasons, the selection of Los Angeles, as opposed to the novel's San Francisco setting, is revealing. In the "four years before the release of *Blade Runner*, 75,000 manufacturing jobs in the region were lost to plant shutdowns and indefinite layoffs, while ten of the twelve largest non-defence-related employers entirely ceased their manufacturing operations in southern California" (Soja 201). In the early 1980s, a "pool of undocumented workers – an estimated 100,000 of whom [were] concentrated in downtown Los Angeles" were used "to weaken unions and drive wages still lower" (McNamara 428). American workers and managers in California faced fears of falling that are registered throughout the action across Harrison Ford's traumatized, angst-ridden face – fears that the film seems problematically content to exacerbate.

V. Conclusion: *Blade Runner's* Class Consciousness

The influx of immigrants in the film, for instance, has obviously not resulted in a healthy multicultural workforce, but rather in a form of "diversity based on segregation, a confluence of rejects and outcasts, the wretched of the earth" (Mueller 45). Here we encounter what might be the ideological limit of Scott's images of miserable masses: the film appears to be suggesting that immigration will convert American metropolises into sites of urban squalor. But perhaps the film is relying on existing anxieties to make a more progressive point: namely, that global capitalism will lead not to a classless utopia, but to a deprived monoclass. Its distinct cultures will blend together like the "mish-mash" of languages that comprise the "city speak" in which they do business, and worse, it will remain dominated by a miniscule elite, a polarization that leaves little space for

Deckard, Bryant, Gaff, and the dwindling number of others caught in between.

If we put any stock in the latter possibility – that the film is critiquing the corporate organization of societies into dominant elite and deprived subaltern classes – it is important that Scott's speculative city is a decaying and dangerous place before the replicants arrive. Most people with the means have left: circling blimps, targeting the wealthy inhabitants of the high-rises, advertise (in English) "the chance to begin again in a land of opportunity and adventure." On the high-rises themselves, targeting the groundlings below, a "'Japanese simulacrum'...which alternates a seductive Japanese face and Coca Cola sign" advertises (in Japanese) various ways to cope with life on Earth (Bruno 186). That is, the "beautiful, richly dressed, exquisitely made-up female Oriental [is] connected in the film (directly or indirectly) with emigration, Coca Cola and pill popping, various forms of consumption, pacification and flight" (Wood 223). We, however, should not conflate the advertising here: the blimps high above promote emigration and literal flight to the wealthy; the electronic billboards below promote consumption and pacification (figurative flight) to the poor who roam the streets, with the clear suggestion that some people can leave, but others must stay. Furthermore, the "go West" rhetoric, and the ostensible promise of peace and opportunity in the off-world colonies, is noteworthy. After all, a "paramilitary force" maintains order in Los Angeles, perhaps suggesting past race or labor riots (Lev 37). Contending with violence, pollution, and few economic opportunities, we might wonder why anyone of sufficient means, like Deckard, would remain.

As the borders separating Deckard from the human and replicant working classes break down throughout the narrative, it becomes clearer that, like them, he has no means of escape and no choice. His fierce drive to make his time on Earth as comfortable as possible is motivated by a fear of falling that is strong enough to enroll him in the fight against the "little people" in order to avoid joining them as an unemployed policeman. However, despite the fact that bonds between replicants and humans are never meant to form, the work of the aptly-named Blade Runners, which aims to sever all connections between humans and their disobedient creations, becomes impossible. And although their function as "detective[s] is precisely to dissolve the impasse of this universalized, free-floating guilt by localizing it in a single subject, thus exculpating all others," they fail (Zizek 59). No real villain is identified, not even the replicants' creator, Tyrell (Joe Turkel), a genetic engineer and cybernetics tycoon whom the film represents as yet another alienated soul, sitting sleeplessly on his bed in his palatial room, playing a solitary game of chess while trading stocks on his computer – his pacifier of choice.

The guilt for the impoverished state of society circulates, therefore, in ways that even implicate our hero, who, before quitting, expertly served the repressive state apparatus and returns to serve it out of fear. Furthermore, as numerous other articles discuss (see Kuhn, e.g.), Deckard comes to love Rachael, a replicant; moreover, he and his nemesis, the replicant Roy, become uncanny doubles. As Deckard hangs from the beam of a skyscraper with his broken hand losing grip, the *mise-en-scène* stages his fear of falling literally. In order not to fall, however, Deckard must renounce his hostility toward his other and instead place faith in him. In a Christ-like act of charity and "human" compassion, Roy saves Deckard's life in the final moments of his own, by lifting him to safety. In this climactic rooftop scene, which echoes the opening skyline shot and frames the narrative, Deckard and Roy stare at each other in a different type of eye exam after realizing that, in effect, both of them are slaves. Rather than seeking out difference in order to eradicate it, however, the gaze here, exchanged between man and machine, middle class bureaucrat-enforcer and working class laborer, results in identification. The film even contains repeated hints that Deckard is, himself, a replicant – why, for instance, has he remained on Earth? How does the Mexican, Gaff, predict his movements and know his fantasies in advance? If the replicants' childhood pictures are fabrications, intended to provide emotional stability, why not Deckard's, too? Because of these points of identification, the tacit boundaries between the classes that comprise American society are allegorically scrutinized in *Blade Runner*, which depicts them being policed in a violent, grotesque form.

Despite the fact that Deckard never "joins the replicant revolution," a scenario in which the film's class critique *should* culminate, according to Robin Wood, *Blade Runner* does more than exaggerate anxieties about undocumented or foreign workers taking American livelihoods (227). And despite its irresolvable plot and, in the end, somewhat ambivalent critique of American capitalism, this allegorical narrative nonetheless questions – perhaps without breaching – the borders between society's dominant and subservient groups, and will continue to occupy a unique place in American popular culture as a recession-era vision of the future.

122

Note

1. Alcohol plays an important but critically disregarded role in *Blade Runner*. Liquor pacifies Deckard in four key scenes: in their first meeting, quoted above, Bryant offers Deckard whiskey, which he quickly shoots back when he anticipates Deckard's resistance to the job offer. When Deckard visits the strip club where Zhora works, he threatens its owner with a fine. Clearly to pacify Deckard and fend off his threats, the owner supplies him with liquor. This exchange appears routine for both men. Moments later, after Deckard has violently "retired" Zhora by shooting her in the back, Bryant notices that Deckard is traumatized and implores him to "drink some for me." And finally, Deckard's domestic life is depicted as a liquor-induced haze during which he numbs his fatigued body, gazes down on the poor groundlings, and nostalgically plays the piano. If Deckard is a replicant, liquor may well be a control mechanism written into his program.

Works Cited

Benjamin, Walter. *Illuminations*. New York: Schocken, 1988.
Blade Runner. Dir. Ridley Scott. Warner Brothers and The Ladd Company, 1982.
Bruno, Giuliana. "Ramble City: Postmodernism and Blade Runner." *Alien Zone*. Ed. Annette Kuhn. London: Verso, 1995. 183-195.
Byers, Thomas B. "Commodity Futures." *Alien Zone*. Ed. Annette Kuhn. London: Verso, 1995. 39-50.
Chow, Rey. *Writing Diaspora: Tactics of Intervention in Contemporary Cultural Studies*. Bloomington: Indiana UP, 1993.
Ehrenreich, Barbara. *Fear of Falling*. New York: Perennial, 1990.
Fancher, Hampton. *Blade Runner*. First published draft. Burbank: Script City, 1981.
Foucault, Michel. *Discipline and Punish*. New York: Penguin, 1997.
Green, David. "Classified Subjects." *Ten* 8.14 (1984): 30-37.
Herman, Judith. *Trauma and Recovery: The Aftermath of Violence – From Domestic Abuse to Political Terror*. New York: Basic Books, 1992.
Harvey, David. *The Condition of Postmodernity*. Oxford: Basil Blackwell, 1989.
Jameson, Frederic. "Postmodernism and Consumer Society." *The Anti-Aesthetic*. Ed. Hal Foster. Port Townsend: Bay Press, 1983. 111-125.
Lev, Peter. "Whose Future: Star Wars, Alien and Blade Runner." *Literature/Film Quarterly* 26.1 (1998): 30-44.
McNamara, Kevin R. "Blade Runner's Post-Individual Worldspace." *Contemporary Literature* 38 (2000): 422-446.
Russell, David. "'I'm Not Gonna Hurt You': Legal Penetrations in Thelma and Louise." *Americana: The Journal of American Popular Culture* 1.1 (2002). < http://www.americanpopularculture.com/journal/articles

/spring_2002/russell.htm>.

Soja, Edward W. *Postmetropolis: Critical Studies of Cities and Regions*. Malden: Blackwell Publishers, 2000.

Tasker, Yvonne. "Approaches to the New Hollywood." *Cultural Studies and Communications*. Eds. James Curran, David Morley, and Valerie Walkerdine. London: Arnold, 1996. 213-238.

Veenhoven, Ruut, and Aldi Hagenaars, eds. *Did the crisis really hurt? Effects of the 1980 - 1982 economic recession on satisfaction, mental health and mortality*. Rotterdam, Netherlands: U of Rotterdam P, 1989.

Wood, Robin. "Papering the Cracks: Fantasy and Ideology in the Reagan Era." *Movies and Mass Culture*. Ed. John Belton. New Brunswick, NJ: Rutgers UP, 1996. 203-228.

Zizek, Slavoj. *Looking Awry: An Introduction to Jacques Lacan through Popular Culture*. Cambridge, MA: The MIT Press, 1991.

124

7

"I'm Not Gonna Hurt You":
Legal Penetrations in *Thelma and Louise*

David Russell

A decade after making their first appearance in American movie theaters, Thelma (Geena Davis) and Louise (Susan Sarandon) continue to cause trouble. Indeed, their names have entered popular culture as shorthand for women engaged in overt criminality. For example, Houston-area police invoked Thelma and Louise as the role models for four young women, all from well-to-do families, who had committed a series of crimes and had taken to calling themselves "queens of armed robbery."[1] In some sense, this appropriation represents the latest in a series of efforts to limit the meaning of Thelma and Louise and their "outlawry." But in refusing to "act like ladies," Thelma and Louise challenge the whole regime of gender as well as the national order predicated upon it. As Judith Butler has argued, "sex" works as a regulatory category, and only the "properly sexed," the "coherent," get recognized as "legitimate" subjects: "In this sense, the category of sex constitutes and regulates what will and will not be an intelligible and recognizable human existence, what will and will not be a citizen capable of rights or speech, an individual protected by law against violence or injury" ("Sexual Inversions" 74). The anxiety evinced by the film's critics and allegorized by the film's male characters, nearly all of whom seek to apprehend and punish these women, shows that a woman's "duty" to her country is to decline personal autonomy and become a site for male privilege and pleasure. Thelma and Louise's "crime," thus, is their effort to generate a new signifying practice and, in the process, expand and reconfigure American citizenship.

Critics of the film, in decrying what they perceived as gratuitous violence, took great pains to connect such excesses to the politics of gender. John Leo of *U.S. News and World Report* called the film's feminism "toxic" (20). Richard Grenier's review in *Commentary* was titled "Killer Bimbos" (50). Writing for *National Review*, John Simon grouped *Thelma and Louise* with films like *Butch Cassidy and the Sundance Kid*, *Easy Rider*, and *Sugarland Express* as "glorification[s] of [apologies] for violence; they pander to piggery, masculine or feminine" (50). Even *Time* columnist Margaret Carlson argued that the film was a setback for feminism: "As a bulletin from the front line in the battle of the sexes, *Thelma and Louise* sends the message that little ground has been won" (57). All of these critics focus on the violence performed by Thelma and Louise and ignore, or at least understate, its underlying causes. That it is women behaving in such a way only seems to add to the horror. Noting that eventually Thelma and Louise take both pride and pleasure in their "gun-slinging outlawry," *Time* film critic Richard Schickel (who reviewed the film positively) suggested, "This is something nice girls – nice people, nice movies – are not supposed to own up to, let alone speak of humorously" (56).

The gist of a great deal of such criticism is that left unpunished, Thelma and Louise represent a significant social threat. For example, in the February 1994 issue of *Playboy*, faux movie critic Joe Bob Briggs ridiculed the film for its stereotypical portrayal of men and called it "nothing more nor less than a great exploitation movie," and he concludes, "I have seen the future, and it has a lot of lesbians in it" (147).[2] Briggs's essay, given its venue and the clearly limited scope of its thinking, could easily be dismissed as inane, yet his argument enacts the very kind of violence upon Thelma and Louise which the various men in the film do. The fact that Louise will not oblige Harlan (Timothy Carhart) and perform oral sex marks her as a "lesbian." The rigidity and myopia of Briggs's categorization puts in clear relief the "crime" they commit – they refuse to be the passive, penetrable bodies that "the law" demands they and all women must be.

On one level, however, Briggs's analysis rings true. *Thelma and Louise* is "a great exploitation film," and it gestures toward the horror films that were its forbearers. For example, the two women plan to go to an isolated cabin for a vacation, a clear reference to the venue of many slasher films. To emphasize this point, Thelma justifies bringing her gun as a defense against any "psycho-killers" they might encounter. The bar where they stop and where Thelma has her ill-fated encounter with Harlan is called The Silver Bullet. Perhaps the least horrific element in this opening sequence is the "monster" Louise kills, but as Carol Clover has noted, the advent of feminism has markedly changed the dynamic of the subgenre of the rape-revenge film: "It is perhaps no accident that the 'masculinization' of the rape victim is accompanied by a 'normalization' of the rapist (that is, the decline of the rapist-as-psychopathic-creep and the rise of the rapist-as-standard-guy)" (Clover 59).[3] As the waitress at The Silver Bullet later tells Detective Slocumb (Harvey Keitel), Harlan was well known as a womanizer. Thus, the audience is left to understand Harlan's actions toward Thelma as "normal" operating procedure and, hence, Louise's action as that of what Clover calls the "Final Girl," the last character in a horror film (usually a woman) who can and does stop the monster. Yet, for the scenario of the "Final Girl" to work, audiences must identify the "monster" as monstrous, something critics like Briggs clearly do not, or will not, do. Clover calls the Final Girl "an agreed upon fiction" that signals a transformation of the slasher genre. "If *Psycho*, like other classic horror films, solves the femininity problem by obliterating the female and replacing her with representatives of the masculine order (mostly but not inevitably males)," Clover argues, "the modern slasher solves it by regendering the woman" (Clover 59). Thus, in Clover's formulation, the Final Girl works to reverse classic gender stereotypes by positing the heroic in the feminine.

However, Harlan, and later, the tanker truck driver, do not produce the same kind of dread as Michael Myers or Jason or Leatherface, at least not in a male audience. In fact, Briggs places Thelma and Louise with the "monsters," facetiously remarking that "[Leatherface] had the moral advantage of being crazy" (147). By moving the "horror" into the register of gender relations, *Thelma and Louise* provokes gender identity reification, not cross-gender identification. Thelma and Louise thus become criminals, not heroes, and their criminality can be redressed only by the reinstitution of "appropriate" gender borders. In exposing the horror of the law of gender, *Thelma and Louise* demands that the audience encounter violence stripped of the veneer of the fantastic.

Thus, Briggs's crude categorization is also violent because it rejects possibilities for identity not accounted for in (and thereby regulated by) the norm of heterosexuality. Briggs "knows" a "lesbian" – a woman who does not act like a woman. This failure to act "appropriately" is precisely Thelma's "crime" against Harlan. "I'm not gonna hurt you," he remarks somewhat incongruously when the two have gone to the parking lot for air. "I just want to kiss you." Thelma's resistance produces physical violence. Harlan slaps Thelma in the face and repeats his previous

promise, now even more incongruous: "I said I'm not gonna hurt you."
When Thelma slaps back, Harlan assaults her. Thelma's "lesbianism"
requires punishment. Harlan rejects any possible understanding of Thelma
that would deny his privilege, and he maintains his "reading" even when
Louise intervenes, telling her that he and Thelma (now bleeding and
crying) were simply "having a little fun."

So begins the mission of Thelma and Louise. Rather than submit
to such a reading practice and the limits it imposes, these characters
attempt a series of semiotic corrections through violence. Louise rejects
Harlan's definition of fun: "In the future, when a woman's crying like that,
she isn't having any fun." Despite Louise holding a gun on him, Harlan
denies her claim. Only men, Harlan seems to believe, can determine
representational legitimacy. Louise's murder of Harlan is her appropriation
of representational violence. "You watch your mouth, buddy," Louise
admonishes after she has shot him. As critic Ann Putnam suggests, Louise
uses violence "to obliterate the awesome silencing power of proprietary
language" (295).

Still, Louise recognizes that her transgression will provoke a swift
response from the state. She rejects Thelma's suggestion to turn
themselves in because, under the auspices of the law, Harlan's crime was
no crime at all:

> THELMA: Shouldn't we go to the cops? I mean, I think we ought
> to tell the police.
> LOUISE: Tell them what, Thelma? Just what do you think we
> should tell them?
> THELMA: I don't know, just tell them what happened.
> LOUISE: Which part?
> THELMA: All of it – that, that he was raping me.
> LOUISE: Just that about a hundred goddamn people saw you
> dancing cheek to cheek with him all night. Who's gonna believe
> that? We don't live in that kind of world, Thelma.

Later, when Thelma asks, "So this is all my fault, is it?" Louise's silence
speaks the position the law encourages her to have – blame the victim. Just
as inflexible gender taxonomies designate "appropriate" and
"inappropriate" subjects, the law posits a representational schema that
permits a similar differentiation. Thelma's impeachable credibility,
impeachable because of her "inappropriate" conduct, makes Harlan's

crime not a crime, at least not in a prosecutable way. Louise's crime is the only one, legally speaking, available for investigation and punishment. As Thelma remarks, in what might be thought of as a summary of one of the film's main themes, "The law is some tricky shit."[4]

Despite Thelma's insistence on bringing in the law, Louise resists, choosing instead to become an outlaw and head for Mexico. Louise's refusal to submit to the law creates a fissure that the law enforcers of the film seek to redress. This "outlawry" opens a space for a subversive representational practice, one in which categorizations of all sorts get deconstructed, but no "norm" is substituted in or privileged. As Elizabeth V. Spelman and Martha Minow have suggested in their analysis of the film, "The price of being protected by the law in court is to surrender control over the telling of your story. Its rich, complicated, and confusing textures are not digestible by the legal record" (275). The film, thus, becomes the alternative to the "legal record," and Thelma and Louise opt to tell their own stories. But these stories are not neat, linear narratives in which every mystery is solved and a happy ending is assured. Instead, these stories are the initial steps toward a signifying practice grounded in "incoherency" and possibility, not taxonomies of gender that are a *fait accompli*.

The violence in the film can and should be seen not as merely gratuitous but as the necessary first step for being heard and acknowledged. Richard Schickel quotes Barbara Bunker, psychology professor at SUNY-Buffalo, as claiming that violent assertiveness is "basically unrestrained expressiveness" (Schickel 56). Thelma and Louise themselves recognize the unexpectedly creative power of violence. After initially escaping the massive police pursuit near the Grand Canyon, Thelma jokingly reflects, "I guess I went a little crazy." Louise responds, "You've always been a little crazy. This is just the first chance you've ever had to really express yourself." Thelma's "craziness" starkly contrasts with her initial appearance when, after yelling to her husband Darryl (Christopher McDonald) that she would answer the phone, she is admonished to keep her voice down. She converses with Louise in a barely audible whisper for fear Darryl will overhear and deny her permission to go on vacation. Thelma begins the film as the quintessential "nice girl," a role that entails her being victimizable, "sane," quiet.

Yet Thelma and Louise's embracing of outlawry and its requisite "craziness" signifies more than mere bloodlust. In their excess, Thelma and Louise enact what Lauren Berlant has deemed "diva citizenship," an effort to display the limits of traditional American personhood and to seek change:

> Diva Citizenship occurs when a person stages a dramatic coup in a public sphere in which she does not have privilege. Flashing up and startling the public, she puts the dominant story into suspended animation; as though recording an estranging voice-over to a film we have all already seen, she renarrates the dominant history as one that the abjected people have once lived sotto voce, but no more; and she challenges her audience to identify with the enormity of the suffering she has narrated and the courage she has had to produce, calling on people to change the social and institutional practices of citizenship to which they currently consent. (Berlant, *The Queen of America* 223)

Thelma and Louise inhabit those roles traditionally occupied by men in order to shock, but in the shock comes the recognition of the limits of sexual and national representation. Thelma's new expressiveness combats her previous *sotto voce* status. The ultimate project of Thelma and Louise is nothing less than the destruction of the taxonomies that sustain the law of the father/nation.

In fact, critics like Joe Bob Briggs recognize all too well the ramifications of such an endeavor, so they respond as a kind of police force themselves, identifying the "enemy," so it can be attacked and destroyed. Lynda Hart anticipates critics like Briggs when she writes, "When the two women in the representation work with rather than against each other, the potentiality for their aggression connoting lesbianism is almost unavoidable" (442). Actions that if performed by Robert Redford and Paul Newman would seem "normal" do not wear as well when performed by Geena Davis and Susan Sarandon. This incongruity, Hart asserts, puzzles audiences: "The anxiety these films generate will be in proportion to the incoherencies in the narrative that permit some glimmer of this recognition" (442).

The "lesbian future" that horrifies Briggs would mean the denial of the primacy of the phallus and, of course, the "laws" premised on such a primacy. The film models this very same male horror as Detective Slocumb, his compatriot from the FBI, and Darryl watch a videotape of Thelma's armed robbery of a convenience store. Each looks on in befuddlement and, not surprisingly, mutters a version of the name of the

Father ("My God!" "Jesus Christ!" "My Lord!"). From this point on, Thelma and Louise go from being a mere curiosity to being dangerous felons, and the law goes into ultimate attack mode.

Thus, through their "incoherent" behavior, Thelma and Louise challenge the state. But their rebellion also challenges the seemingly coherent category of gender by denying the psychoanalytical truism of woman as "lack" and penetrability as normative. Under such a regime, women can be subject to the law – that is, take their "proper" place in the heterosexual matrix – only by acquiring a substitute: "No matter how much 'felt experience' of her uterus and vagina the little girl has...the fact remains that she cannot see it and is reduced to imagining it (that is, to imagining herself...), with the help of the boy's erect phallus" (Borch-Jacobsen 216). Put another way, only by being penetrated can women "imagine themselves." Refusing penetration as a necessary component for producing their "correct" subjectivity puts women at odds with "the law."

Refusing penetration also confounds male privilege and necessitates a reassertion of "the law" and a return to normalcy. "At best [women] may obey Law itself, the law of the same, which requires that the little girl abandon her relation to the origin and her primal fantasy so that henceforth she can be inscribed into those of men which will become the 'origin' of her desire," Luce Irigaray argues, critiquing Freudian/Lacanian discourse. "In other words, woman's only relation to origin is one dictated by man's. She is crazy, disoriented, lost, if she fails to join in this first male desire" (Irigaray 33). Having rejected "the law" and refused to confess, Thelma and Louise broach the possibility of "illegal" trajectories of desire. In their actions, they propose a new signifying practice, indeed, a new signifying economy, that rejects "lack" and the necessity of female penetration. These actions mark them as "crazy, disoriented, lost," a fact they celebrate, but the men in the film fear and use as a justification for their pursuit. Thus, the setting for the final scenes of the film must be understood as the staging of this new practice – the Grand Canyon, a "hole," an absence, a "lack" that so many come to "see."

Once they fully embrace the possibilities of their outlawhood, Thelma and Louise consistently reject the primacy of the phallus. For example, critics have generally recognized their destruction of the tanker truck as an attack on a giant penis. But that violence is merely the culmination of an attack that begins in language. Having already asked if they were "ready for a big d---," the trucker makes the opening gambit in a game that he has apparently played many times before, yet Thelma and

Louise refuse to play by "the rules." Instead, they chastise him for his "bad manners" and purposely misread his various obscene gestures. Louise asks, "And all that...pointing to your lap – I mean, what is that supposed to mean exactly? I mean, does it mean, 'Pull over, I want to show you what a big fat slob I am'?" In the same way that Harlan refused to read his treatment of Thelma as an assault, Louise refuses to acknowledge the phallic superiority of the truck driver. She reads lack where the trucker sees power. Utterly befuddled by his reception, the trucker articulates the idea that by now so many men in the movie (and in the theaters) have of Thelma and Louise: "You women are crazy!" Far from denying it, Louise gleefully asserts, "Got that right!"

At the same time that Thelma and Louise confound phallocentric law, they also make themselves impenetrable. In her encounter with J.D. (Brad Pitt), Thelma learns the pitfalls of penetrability. Their sexual intimacy gives J.D. the opportunity to steal Louise's getaway money. Moreover, once captured, J.D. tells Slocumb about Thelma and Louise's escape plans. "You've just gotta stop talking to people," Louise admonishes Thelma. "You've got to stop being open."

Perhaps because of the mysterious events in Texas, Louise understands better than Thelma the benefits of being impenetrable. At the beginning of the film, she waits on two young women who are smoking. "You girls are kinda young to be smoking, don't you think?" she asks. Then she adds, "Ruins your sex drive." In the very next scene, Louise herself lights up a cigarette and calls not her boyfriend but Thelma, the woman she intends to leave town with. As Louise later tells a male co-worker, "[Thelma's] running away with me." When her boyfriend Jimmy (Michael Madsen) arrives in Oklahoma City with the money for her and Thelma's getaway, their encounter in the hotel room does not involve sex (at least not on screen). Later, when Detective Slocumb urges Louise to turn herself in or risk death, Louise responds with a curious litany: "You know, certain words and phrases just keep drifting through my mind, things like incarceration, cavity search, death by electrocution, life imprisonment." The conflation of penetration with "incarceration" and "death" underscores what Louise sees as the ultimate result of submitting to the law.

As Louise conveys to Thelma, impenetrability requires silence. In fact, Louise refuses to discuss a great deal with Thelma, the police, and, by default, the audience, beginning with the mysterious events in Texas. Lynda Hart suggests that by "resisting divulging her secret, Louise becomes 'the criminal,' and it is thus just as much what she refuses to say as what she has done that criminalizes her" (Hart 434). Louise resists making herself "knowable." She offers no *mea culpa* for the death of Harlan, and she provides no insight that might make her "criminality" understandable. In failing to confess, Louise confounds the "truth" seekers who wish to verify the law and her place in it.[5]

The "craziness," "incoherence," and "impenetrability" that mark Thelma and Louise as "bad" women also mark them as "bad" citizens. With the notable exception of Slocumb, all of the law enforcement officers in the film see the two women as dangerous criminals. As the army of police encircles Thelma and Louise at the end of the film, the officer in charge demands that they throw down their weapons and turn off the engine of the car. "Any failure to obey that command will be considered an act of aggression against us," he asserts. Of course, the whole film has been an act of disobedience (coded as "aggression") against the law. In pleading with his FBI colleague for leniency, Slocumb sees the snipers at the ready and asks, "How many times do these women have to be f-----over?" The question itself evokes the penetrative logic of psychoanalytic discourse and highlights the fact that the state maintains the same stance. At the end, "the law" is in the same position as Harlan at The Silver Bullet – ready to "f---" these women and feel perfectly justified in doing so. Slocumb's realization comes too late to help Thelma and Louise, but his running toward them, away from his law enforcement colleagues, is a powerful rejection of what the law symbolizes throughout the film.

The over-the-top nature of the law's reaction demonstrates the anxiety provoked by female outlawry. "All of this for us," Thelma marvels as she watches the pursuit. "The unrestrained body is a statement or a language about unrestrained morality," historian Bryan S. Turner theorizes. "To control women's bodies is to control their personalities, and represents an act of authority over the body in the interests of public order organized around male values of what is rational" (197). Thelma and Louise exceed the parameters of acceptable citizenship, and the state must respond by restoring "order." Left "unrestrained," the two would embody an alternative practice of citizenship that would challenge not just the law but the very definition of "freedom."

Their "unrestrained bodies" also threaten the core of constitutional personhood. By determining for themselves how their bodies will signify, Thelma and Louise also control how (and if) their bodies will be seen at all. The success of their outlawry relies on their ability to stay out of sight.

Critic Lauren Berlant argues that power inheres in abstraction: "The white, male body is the relay to legitimization, but even more than that, the power to suppress that body, to cover its tracks and its traces, is the sign of real authority, according to constitutional fashion" ("National Brands/National Body" 113). Berlant suggests that those members of the populace unable to suppress their bodies, women and people of color in particular, become targets for repression because of their very embodiment. White men, by contrast, enjoy the privilege of abstraction. Thus, Thelma and Louise can be assaulted because their bodies deny them full citizenship and bespeak an inherent vulnerability. The murder of Harlan shocks the system by removing the veneer of abstraction for white males and positing in its place vulnerability, "lack." This counterpenetration demands a resignification of national embodiment and, as a result, of just who counts as a "citizen" as well.[6]

One method Thelma and Louise employ to further problematize the distinctions of the "law" (male/female, citizen/criminal, etc.) is a constant re-dressing. They remake themselves through creative borrowing and transvestic trade with men, in the process showing the creative possibilities of interchangeable, capacious subjectivities. "Something's crossed over in me, and I can't go back," Thelma proclaims when she fears Louise might abandon her. "I mean, I just couldn't live."

Rejecting their old "restrained" selves, both women divest themselves of the signifiers of that lawful personhood. For instance, as she waits while Thelma robs the convenience store, Louise begins to apply some lipstick but, after seeing some townswomen looking at her, she tosses it out of the car. Later, she trades her jewelry to an elderly man at a roadside stop for his cowboy hat. Prior to locking the overly officious highway patrolman in the trunk of his squad car, Louise exchanges her sunglasses for his while Thelma holds him at gunpoint.

Like Louise, Thelma "re-dresses" as well, though her borrowing focuses less on clothing and more on identity options. For example, early in the film, Thelma takes one of Louise's cigarettes and, looking at herself in the side mirror, says, "I'm Louise." Even at this early stage, Thelma recognizes the inadequacy of her "place" as Darryl's wife. Later, after J.D. has made off with their money, Thelma adopts the script he has given her and robs the convenience store.[7] Thelma's surprising ability as an outlaw (at one point, she brags to Louise, "I believe I have a knack for this shit!") also highlights the "crossing over" into a previously male domain.

Marjorie Garber has argued that transvestism functions as a "third," which disrupts binaries and causes "category crisis." In this way, transvestism must be seen, in Garber's judgment, as "a space of possibility structuring and confounding culture: the disruptive element that intervenes, not just a category crisis of male and female, but the crisis of category itself" (Garber 17). Such a disruption has implications for various "laws" outlining normative behaviors:

> By "category crisis" I mean a failure of definitional distinction, a borderline that becomes permeable, that permits of border crossings from one (apparently distinct) category to another: black/white, Jew/Christian, noble/bourgeois, master/servant, master/slave. The binarism male/female, one apparent ground of distinction (in contemporary eyes, at least) between "this" and "that," "him" and "me," is itself put in question or under erasure in transvestism, and a transvestite figure, or a transvestite mode, will always function as a sign of overdetermination – a mechanism of displacement from one blurred boundary to another. (Garber 17)

For Garber, popular culture is too quick to recoup the transvestite figure and assign him/her to a specific gender category. However, the presence of "a transvestite mode" does not merely signify a crisis in the category of gender. Rather, it highlights other crises, crises that can be elided by focusing on the seemingly aberrant nature of the transvestite (read as "criminal" in certain contexts).

Thelma and Louise, in some sense, enacts a "transvestite mode" throughout. Susan Sarandon and Geena Davis "play" the roles that Robert Redford and Paul Newman (or any other "buddy" or road picture pairing) had previously occupied. Thus, the film does concern itself with a crisis in gender taxonomy. However, it also plays through the crisis of American citizenship. Thelma and Louise try to escape the border of the nation, but they would not have to cross that border were the parameters of citizenship more capacious and welcoming of multiple subject positions. The one piece of clothing Thelma takes from a man is the baseball cap of the tanker truck driver. After destroying the tanker, Thelma scoops up a dirty baseball cap with a dingy American flag on it. In her own project of resignification, Thelma appropriates the national symbol from a man and makes it her own. For a brief moment, the outlaw is America. Significantly, though, when the law moves in on the two women, their new hats blow off in a gust of wind from the FBI helicopter. Thus, law reestablishes "order."

Shortly before their capture, Thelma confides to Louise, "I feel awake, wide awake. Everything looks different. You feel like that, too, like you've got something to look forward to?" This last question is ironic given that only a few minutes later they are trapped. Yet, their decision to "keep going," to drive off the cliff, is a triumph of sorts. In a gesture toward the work of theorists like Butler, Lauren Berlant concedes that various performative strategies have the effect of re-privileging the body of the "other"; yet she also asserts, "But sometimes a person doesn't want to seek the dignity of an always-already-violated body, and wants to cast hers off, either for nothingness, or in a trade for some other, better model" ("National Brands/National Bodies" 114). Thelma and Louise initially opt for the "better model" of outlawhood, and, in doing so, they confuse and terrify the men they encounter. When the law closes in on them, however, they refuse to assume their prescribed identities. Having already confessed that they "can't live" the old way, they accept "nothingness" rather than apprehension. In the new economy of desire that Thelma and Louise have glimpsed and tried to live, the canyon into which they leap is the beginning, not the end of their narrative. As Butler herself has argued, "Perhaps only by risking the incoherence of identity is connection possible" (*The Psychic Life of Power* 149). By denying the law its final triumph and through their gestures of love toward one another, Thelma and Louise become patriots in a new revolution, that of activating and celebrating various identity positions outside the law. Signification without representation becomes a tyranny worth fighting against.

Putting into perspective the controversy created by her film, screenwriter Callie Khouri noted in a 1997 interview that "a lot of people are very sensitive and like their violence in a very particular way: male on male or male on female" (Bowers 74). The "crimes" committed by Thelma and Louise result from the reversal of that trajectory of violence. Thelma and Louise challenge the contours of citizenship and gender with their outlawry, but they also show that the fiction of nation and the unity that fiction implies rely upon violence against women, particularly a reliance on their penetrability. These "criminals" also show that the law will code as deviant that which it cannot comprehend. The production of such "criminality" thus becomes one of the chief methods by which the nation affirms itself, its borders, and its "rightful" subjects. In refusing to go away, Thelma and Louise hold out an alternative national and sexual signifying practice that truly could be called "democratic."

Notes

1. For a discussion of the media frenzy surrounding these young women, see Max J. Robins. Ironically, on the page following this story was a picture of pop star Britney Spears, bare midriffed. A short summary of a then upcoming MTV special featuring Spears begins, "Talk about a body in motion." The juxtaposition, though perhaps coincidental, nonetheless demonstrates "appropriate" and "inappropriate" uses for the young female body.

2. A more "legitimate" academic critic who argues the same basic point is Richard A. Schwartz. He argues that the film resembles Shakespearean tragedies like *Hamlet* in that "the film's tragic power stems from the interplay between our desires for the protagonists' success and well being and our intensifying expectations that the preservation of law and order will require their demise" (102-3). Schwartz later asserts that the police officers in the film are "generally positive figures who act professionally" and that viewers (whom Schwartz refers to as "we") "never question the appropriateness of their pursuing the fugitives" (105).

3. Carol J. Clover herself acknowledges the connection between *Thelma and Louise* and such critically despised rape-revenge films as *I Spit on Your Grave*, but she also perceives *Thelma and Louise* as "a very, very safe film" because of the presence of Slocumb, a male character the audience can identify with. Though Slocumb seems to understand the plight of the women better than any other member of law enforcement, he also doggedly pursues both and, in fact, is instrumental in their capture by keeping Louise on the phone long enough to be traced. As I will argue, the film itself contradicts Clover's conflation of "safety" with "the law" throughout, and Slocumb's sympathy with Thelma and Louise does not stop him from doing his job in the way, for example, that "Dirty" Harry Callahan refuses to arrest the woman exacting revenge on her and her sister's rapists in *Sudden Impact*.

4. In *Toward a Feminist Theory of the State*, Catherine MacKinnon points out that with questions of rape, women are often faced with such representational dilemmas: "From women's point of view, rape is not prohibited; it is regulated. Even women who know they have been raped do not believe that the legal system will see it the way they do. Often they are not wrong" (179). This "regulation" produces the mindset that women's bodies are not their own but rather a form of community property. The law produces a representational practice that allows the female body to signify only in ways that elide male criminality, except in the most extreme of cases.

5. In Volume I of *The History of Sexuality*, Michel Foucault argues that the act of

confessing in western culture has become imbued with the aura of truth-telling, particularly when it comes to questions of sex. Confession, thus, leads to "freedom." Indeed Detective Slocumb promises Louise that if she will simply confess, he will do everything in his power to "help" her and Thelma. Oddly, though, Slocumb does not seem to need Louise's confession. He "knows" what has happened, and he even tells Louise that he knows what happened to her in Texas. Slocumb thus seeks a confession not for the "truth" but for his prosecution. Foucault suggests that confession always serves to confirm power: "[T]he agency of domination does not reside in the one who speaks (for it is he who is constrained), but in the one who listens and says nothing; not in the one who knows and answers, but in the one who questions and is not supposed to know. And this discourse of truth finally takes effect, not in the one who receives it, but in the one from whom it is wrested" (62). Louise sagely realizes that confession will not lead to freedom but rather to a reinscription in the mechanisms of power.

6. Working from Berlant's ideas as well as the writings of Ludwig Wittgenstein, Thomas E. Yingling adds people with AIDS to the category of those whose bodies preclude them from full citizenship. Agreeing with Berlant's assessment of bodily abstraction as political empowerment, Yingling points out that commodified male bodies such as Arnold Schwarzenegger and Sylvester Stallone show that the body itself is easily overcome in the service of sustaining an idealized masculinity: "Wounds do not identify the body as a surface inscribed by history; rather, they serve as a measure of triumph, an index of the distance traveled in transcendence. The male body suffers in these texts, but 'real men' rise above it" (29). Thus, Louise's murder of Harlan upsets the possibility of such idealization. Not only can Harlan not transcend his body, but he fails to utilize Thelma's body for the pleasure that the law claims he is entitled to. By allowing himself to be penetrated (by a woman, no less), Harlan evinces a malaise of citizenship that the law cannot countenance.

7. Lillian S. Robinson suggests that Thelma adopts J.D.'s persona. Robinson notes that after robbing the convenience store, Thelma's bodily demeanor changes dramatically: "Her movements (and almost her body itself) become more streamlined, more controlled and inner-directed. She is not only boyish, she is like the particular boy who showed her how – and who, ironically enough, in giving her what Louise calls the first 'proper lay' of her life, would conventionally be supposed to have 'made her a woman'" (188). Thelma's bodily comportment reflects her new "impenetrable" self, but Robinson also points out that using J.D. as a model presages an eventual fall for Thelma. When J.D. is captured by the police, he is "feminized": "The only person who has less real power than the smart-mouthed working class boy is, in fact, almost any working-class girl or woman" (188).

Works Cited

Berlant, Lauren. "National Brands/National Body: Imitation of Life." *Comparative American Identities: Race, Sex and Nationality in the Modern Text*. Ed. Hortense Spillers. New York: Routledge, 1991. 110-140.

---. *The Queen of America Goes to Washington City*. Durham: Duke UP, 1997.

Borch-Jacobsen, Mikkel. *Lacan: The Absolute Master*. Stanford: Stanford UP, 1991.

Bowers, Michelle. "Thelma and Louise Debuts." *Entertainment Weekly* 23 May 1997: 74.

Briggs, Joe Bob. "Mantrack." *Playboy* 41(2) 1994: 35+.

Butler, Judith. "Sexual Inversions." *Feminist Interpretations of Michel Foucault*. Ed. Susan J. Hekman. University Park, Pennsylvania: The Pennsylvania State UP, 1996. 59-75.

---. *The Psychic Life of Power: Theories of Subjection*. Stanford: Stanford UP, 1997.

Carlson, Margaret. "Is This What Feminism is All About?" *Time* 24 June 1991: 57.

Clover, Carol J. *Men, Women, and Chain Saws*. Princeton: Princeton UP, 1992.

Foucault, Michel. *The History of Sexuality, Volume I*. New York: Vintage Books,1990.

Garber, Marjorie. *Vested Interests: Cross-Dressing and Cultural Anxiety*. New York: HarperPerennial, 1992.

Grenier, Richard. "Killer Bimbos." *Commentary* September 1991: 50+.

Hart, Lynda. "Til Death Do Us Part: Impossible Spaces in Thelma and Louise." *Journal of the History of Sexuality* 4 (1994): 430-446.

Irigaray, Luce. *Speculum of the Other Woman*. Ithaca: Cornell UP, 1985.

Leo, John. "Toxic Feminism on the Big Screen." *U.S. News and World Report* 10 June 1991: 20.

MacKinnon, Catherine. *Toward a Feminist Theory of the State*. Cambridge: Harvard UP, 1989.

Putnam, Ann. "The Bearer of the Gaze in Ridley Scott's Thelma and Louise." *Western American Literature* 27 (1993): 291-302.

Robinson, Lillian S. "Out of the Mine and into the Canyon: Working-Class Feminism, Yesterday and Today." *The Hidden Foundation: Cinema and the Question of Class*. Eds. David E. James and Rick Berg. Minneapolis: U of Minnesota P, 1996. 172-192.

Robins, J. Max. "How Teen Bandit 'Queens' Became Prime-Time Princesses." *TV Guide* 48.20 (2000): 75-76.

Schickel, Richard. "Gender Bender." *Time* 24 June 1991: 56.

Schwartz, Richard A. "The Tragic Vision of Thelma and Louise." *Journal of Evolutionary Psychology* 17 (1996): 101-107.

Simon, John. "Movie of the Moment." *National Review* 8 July 1991: 50.

Spelman, Elizabeth V. and Martha Minow. "Outlaw Women: Thelma and Louise." *Legal Reelism: Movies as Legal Texts.* Ed. John Denvir. Urbana: U of Illinois P, 1996. 261-279.

Thelma and Louise. Dir. Ridley Scott. Warner Brothers. 1991.

Turner, Bryan S. *The Body and Society.* New York: Basil Blackwell Inc., 1984.

Yingling, Thomas E. *AIDS and the National Body.* Durham: Duke UP, 1997.

8

Violence and Masculinity in *Saving Private Ryan*

Vernon Shetley

Steven Spielberg's *Saving Private Ryan* has been one of the most discussed and debated, and one of the most extravagantly praised, movies of recent years. Most mainstream reviewers extolled the brutal realism of its depiction of combat, many suggesting that the film achieves a new and unprecedented kind of authenticity in its representation of the experience of war. Stephen Hunter of the *Washington Post* stated that in "one stroke, it makes everything that came before…seem dated and unwatchable" (B1); David Ansen wrote in *Newsweek* that "Steven Spielberg has taken Hollywood's depiction of war to a new level" (57); Anthony Lane of the *New Yorker* celebrated "what must be the most telling battle scenes ever made" (77).   While *Saving Private Ryan* lost out to the anodyne *Shakespeare in Love* for the best picture Oscar, Spielberg nevertheless collected his second best director award (having previously received the same honor for *Schindler's List*, another World War II era film).   And the film brought in more than $400 million at the box office.

While the mainstream media for the most part lavished praise upon the film, some dissenting voices were heard, many among the right-wing journals of opinion. These critics for the most part acknowledged the power of the combat scenes, but protested the absence of explicit didacticism in the film. Christopher Caldwell, writing for *Commentary*, typified these responses. He granted that *Saving Private Ryan* offered "a powerful and richly textured account of war" (48), but went on to express uneasiness with the film's narrow focus on the dynamics of small-unit combat, its failure to provide a big-picture view that might have made clear the justifications for putting men in danger: "Spielberg's movie *assumes* that its audience knows the reasons why World War II was fought, but any such assumption is fraught with pitfalls. Absent Ike-with-

142

a-pointer, in what way are we witnessing in this movie anything other than cold-blooded, nonsensical mass murder?" (51). John Simon, also in *Commentary*, focused more on cinematic than ideological failings in the film, but came to a similar conclusion; for him, *Saving Private Ryan* is finally "a great exercise in gratuitousness" (52). Both these reviewers wanted the film to point to its moral more explicitly. A few skeptical voices protested not the absence of a moral but the sentimentality that, behind the violence, still saturates Spielberg's vision. Louis Menand, writing in the liberal *New York Review of Books*, and James Bowman, in the right-wing *American Spectator*, both single out the scene at army headquarters in which George Marshall gives the order to retrieve Private Ryan as a particularly egregious example of Spielbergian sentimentality: Menand described it as "beyond Capra" (8), Bowman as "Lincolnian schmaltz" (68).

The mainstream critics tended to focus on the scenes of intense combat that bracket the film, while the skeptics focus on Spielberg's treatment of the moral issue that arises from the mission on which Captain Miller's (Tom Hanks) unit is sent: whether rescuing a single man (so that his bereaved mother is spared further loss) is worth endangering the lives of many more. Louis Menand and Tom Carson are equally dismissive of the film's presentation of this question, though from opposite points of view. Menand asks, rhetorically, "If soldiers do not fight for motherhood, what do they fight for?" (8). Carson is even more impatient: "One reason the onscreen debates about the mission's value go in such circles is that the down-to-earth answer to the movie's big question – is one man's life worth risking eight – is so screamingly obvious: No" (72).

That two exceptionally intelligent critics can come to opposite conclusions about this apparently central point, both insisting that the dilemma the film poses is not a real one and that its answer is obvious, suggests that the movie's moral center of gravity lies elsewhere, that this question functions as a blind to cover the dynamic that is most urgently at work in the film. That dynamic I locate in the film's exploration of the relationship between violence and masculinity. I agree with Menand and Carson that the moral issue of Private Ryan's rescue is empty, but the film indeed puts forward a moral discourse, though little of that discourse is presented discursively, in the form of moral debate. Instead, it is carried out surreptitiously, as it were, largely through narrative means. The film's explicit moral discourse focuses on orders from headquarters, where the Chief of Staff of the U.S. Army is not too busy to take action to assuage a grieving mother's pain. The discourse I will examine turns rather on particular dilemmas that arise for Captain Miller's unit in the field, which turn out to be a good deal more disturbing than the appeal to motherhood that underwrites the film's explicit moral.

I will focus in particular on two incidents in the film, both involving a German soldier who is captured and then released by the Americans. The soldier is captured about midway into the film, in an assault by the unit on a German machine gun nest, to whose presence the American soldiers have been alerted by discovering the body of a dead Allied soldier. Miller's platoon is in favor of bypassing the machine gun emplacement altogether, leaving it for others to deal with, but the Captain insists that it is their responsibility to take out these Germans, lest other Americans be killed by them. In the process of the assault, one of the unit is killed and a German soldier is captured. The enlisted men in the platoon simply assume that they will kill the captured soldier, but the translator, Corporal Upham (Jeremy Davies), who has been plucked from the field equivalent of an office job for the mission, and who has not participated in the fighting, argues that killing a prisoner would be immoral. The American soldiers protest that they cannot take a prisoner with them on their mission, and the German, should he link back up with troops of his own army, might return to fight against the Americans again. Corporal Upham's argument prevails with the Captain, who, despite some misgivings, orders the prisoner released, though this order comes close to precipitating a mutiny among the enlisted men. It seems, for the moment, that decency and civilization, the sort of decency and civilization that insist that shooting a defenseless man with his hands up is never the right thing to do, has prevailed. We understand the baser instincts displayed by the enlisted men, but applaud the way that Upham's scruples have prevented an unconscionable act.

But this is not the last of the story. The platoon goes on, at the end of the movie, to fight another tumultuous engagement, this time to prevent a German detachment from reaching and crossing a bridge. The German soldier who had earlier been spared returns to fight against Miller's band of soldiers, just as the enlisted men had predicted when they argued for killing him. And he fights with great effectiveness, killing Mellish, the one Jewish soldier in Miller's unit, in an extended scene of hand to hand combat, and dropping Captain Miller with a well-placed shot towards the end of this final battle. Upham, on the other hand, is given a simple job, that of ferrying ammunition to the other soldiers, but he is paralyzed by fear, and his failure to do his job contributes directly to the deaths of several of the men. So whatever moral authority we might suppose Upham to have gained in the earlier episode with the prisoner is canceled by his cowardice in the final battle, and the humanistic and intellectual values he has stood for are undermined as well.

The film goes out of its way, in fact, to set itself against Upham's point of view. After the assault on the machine gun nest, in which the unit's medic, Wade, is killed, Mellish grabs Upham and drags him up to the captured German soldier, telling Upham to ask "if he's the one who shot Wade." Upham tells Mellish "it doesn't matter," to which Mellish responds "it *does* matter." At this point in the film, viewers are likely to side with Upham in this argument – who can tell who shot whom in the swirling chaos of the scenes we have witnessed? – and after all, as the German prisoner himself says, "it's war." We understand that Mellish, in the stress of battle, might respond to the loss of a comrade in the way he does, but we share Upham's perspective that it is pointless to personalize the situation of war. However, in the final battle, the film takes great pains to itemize the costs of Upham's compassion. Besides showing the hand-to-hand combat in which the returned German kills Mellish, the film also picks the German out, among a group of soldiers firing with him from the same position, as the one who delivers the fatal wound to Captain Miller. We see him work the action of his rifle, take careful aim, and then, in a reverse shot over his shoulder, witness the shot that brings down the heroic Captain. Upham may not have cared who shot Wade, but the film clearly feels that it is important that we know precisely who killed Captain Miller.

Both Upham and Captain Miller are, in their different ways, intellectuals. They share a moment of closeness at one point, when Miller recognizes that Upham is quoting from Emerson in the course of a conversation. Upham supposes that being in combat, under fire, will provide a kind of spiritual benefit, as Emerson proposes in the sentence Upham quotes: "War educates the senses, calls into action the will, perfects the physical constitution...." Miller, though, while recognizing the quotation, lightly mocks Emerson's idealistic notion of the effects of war, remarking, "I guess that's Emerson's way of finding the bright side." Having witnessed the inferno of Omaha Beach, we share Miller's hardened perspective; Emerson, the film implies, is a naïve egghead, whose words are empty because he knows nothing of the real experience of war. Miller, it turns out, was a schoolteacher in civilian life. But he conceals this fact from his men; the pool to be won by the man who discovers Miller's civilian occupation has grown to $300 by the time Miller himself reveals it. Though both are intellectuals, Miller, unlike Upham, makes no show of bookishness, and unlike Upham, who turns out to be a coward, Miller shows great courage throughout the battles we witness; the film implies a connection between Miller's hiding of his intellectual attainments and his matter-of-fact bravery, and Upham's overt intellectuality and his cowardice.

Upham is attached to ideas, and ideals, and manages to persuade Captain Miller to share those ideals in letting the prisoner go free. But the reappearance of the captured German as a soldier, a fiercely effective killing machine, styled as an almost absurd exaggeration of Aryan power and purity, leads to the conclusion that the enlisted men were right and Upham mistaken in the earlier debate. Upham seems to acknowledge as much in the one act of violence he commits. A *deus ex machina*, the arrival of American reinforcements, saves the day at the end of the film, but only after almost all of Miller's unit, including the Captain himself, have been killed. Upham, who has been hiding throughout the battle, jumps up with a rifle to capture a group of the suddenly outgunned Germans. Finding the man whose life he had argued successfully to save, Upham now shoots him, as the men of the platoon had wished to do earlier. Spielberg leaves the import of this act deliberately ambiguous. Are we to think that Upham has been brutalized by combat and undone by shame over his failure in the battle to the point that he has lost the moral compass that had earlier steered him? Perhaps. But his moral authority has already been undermined by his performance in the battle – men of conscience, it is implied, will turn out to be cowards. The film suggests rather that Upham's original fault lay in the scruples that led him to try to prevent the killing of the German prisoner in the first place, that real men do not let their anguished humanistic values stand in the way of killing an unarmed man with his hands up. In other words, the film implies that the measure of one's manhood is the ability and willingness to kill in cold blood. Masculinity is distinct from, and in fundamental conflict with, one's humanity, and it is better, the film implies, to be masculine than to be humane. After Upham shoots the German, the camera shows us the corporal's face, his eyes clearly filled with a new hardness and resolve; the rest of the surrendering Germans cower back, acknowledging his force and authority. John Simon is true to the spirit of the film when he refers to this moment as Upham's "heroic redemption" (52); Upham is now a man. But it is a peculiar kind of heroism that shows itself in the killing of an unarmed man.

Corporal Upham's masculinity, in question throughout the film, seems to be restored as he takes revenge upon the German soldier on behalf of his dead comrades. I want to focus on one of those dead comrades in particular: Mellish (Adam Goldberg), the only Jewish soldier in the unit. He is distinguished from the others by his being Jewish – the other soldiers in the platoon make nothing of it, but he insists on it himself, in a scene in which he shows the Star of David he wears to a group of captured German soldiers marching past – but also by the intensity of the hints of homoeroticism around this figure (is it an accident that Mellish's nickname among the unit is "Fish"?). Certainly homosexual panic and a latent sense of homoeroticism are constants in war films, in almost any film, in fact, that focuses on interactions among groups of men without women. But Mellish is the soldier around whom suggestions of homoerotic desire gather most forcefully. This is the case almost from the moment when the men are first individualized for us, in their conversation on the initial march of their mission. Captain Miller offers a witty retort to Private Reiben's griping, whereupon Mellish remarks "he's good," and his marching partner, Caparzo. replies, "I love him"; Mellish mimes kisses toward Caparzo, who responds by miming a kiss to Mellish. Homoerotic suggestion is most explicit in the scene that precedes the final battle, in which the Americans, having made their preparations, await the arrival of the German troops. Mellish and Upham listen to an Edith Piaf record on a Victrola; as Upham translates the words of Piaf's love lament, Mellish tells him, "to be honest, I find myself curiously aroused by you." Later, shortly before the arrival of the German troops, when Mellish's partner at his station asks if he has a stick of gum to spare, Mellish takes the wad of gum he is chewing from his mouth, pinches off half of it, and gives that to his partner, an exchange of bodily fluids that seems decidedly suggestive of a kiss.

Keeping in mind this strain of suggestion, Mellish's death is striking and disturbing. He is overcome by the returned prisoner in a lengthy bout of hand to hand combat. At the end of the fight the pair are on the floor, with the German lying on top of the American, both looking directly into one another's eyes, speaking directly to one another. Slowly, the German pushes a bayonet (held at a curiously oblique angle) into Mellish's chest. One reviewer, Thomas Doherty, remarked that this "excruciating duel...plays like an act of coitus" (70). Or perhaps an act of rape. Mellish repeatedly says "stop" as the German bears down to penetrate his chest with the knife, while the German says, "let's end it...it's easier for you like this...it's almost over, it's almost done." The suggestion of rape is reinforced by the shot that follows. The German appears at the head of the stairs, his stature and power enhanced by an almost absurdly low-angle shot, and strides slowly and majestically down, past the sniveling, mewling Upham, whom the German passes by with a look of utter contempt and disdain, the way a lordly gentleman of the manor might pass by a cringing underling after exercising his *droit du seigneur*. Upham, his look implies, is not even worth killing.

The film seems to connect Mellish's failure in this hand-to-hand fight to some femininity in his own character, as opposed to the virile manhood of the commanding German. Homosexuality, then, is linked to weakness, to a deficiency of masculinity, and that deficiency is connected to Jewishness. In fact, we might see Upham and Mellish as a single archetype, split out into two figures through the process that Ernest Jones, in his analysis of *Hamlet*, refers to as "decomposition." Jones indicates by that term one of the "mechanisms of myth formation" in which "various attributes of a given individual are disunited, and several other individuals are invented, each endowed with one group of the original attributes. In this way one person of complex character is dissolved and replaced by several, each of whom possesses a different aspect of the character which in a simpler form of the myth was combined in one being" (131). So, in many fairy tales, the figure of the mother, always a focus of powerful and powerfully ambivalent feeling, is split into a departed "good" mother and an evil stepmother, or in *Hamlet*, the figure of the father is split into the dead father who loves Hamlet and the evil uncle, who sleeps with Hamlet's mother and wishes to kill the prince.

Effeminacy and intellectuality, as Sander Gilman has demonstrated in a series of books, were two of the common stereotypes of anti-Semitic propaganda in the first half of the twentieth century; the Jew was represented as someone whose association with intellectualism was intimately allied to his lack of authentic masculinity. Gilman notes that "'intellectuals' quickly became the Nazi code word for Jews, as it had been in France during the Dreyfus Affair. Thus at the book burning in Berlin on 10 May 1933, Joseph Goebbels was able to announce the end of 'an age of exaggerated Jewish intellectualism'" (83-84). This association of Jews with "intellectualism" was allied to the notion, widespread in nineteenth and twentieth century racial thought, that, for Jews, "superior intelligence is a form of biological compensation" (Gilman 23). Even Jews acknowledged the force of this stereotype to the extent that they felt compelled to call for the redirection of Jewish energies; Kafka's friend Felix Weltsch, in the Prague Zionist journal *Self-Defense*, complained that Jews lack "manliness" and ought to "shed our heavy stress on intellectual preeminence," spending less time "debating" and more time in "play and gymnastics" (Gilman 23).

This idea of the weakness of the Jewish body, and the corresponding overdevelopment of the Jewish mind, went hand in hand with representations of the Jew as feminized. The turn of the century French historian Anatole Leroy-Beaulieu described Jews as having an "unmanly appearance" and endorses the idea that the "Semites are...a feminine race...always lacking in virility and procreative power'" (Gilman 49). Otto Weininger, in his massive pseudo-scientific treatise *Sex and Character* (1903), remarks that "Judaism is saturated with femininity, with precisely those qualities the essence of which I have shown to be in the strongest opposition to the male nature" (306), and that the "Jew is... notably less potent sexually [than the Aryan]" (311). "The most manly Jew," Weininger states, "is more feminine than the least manly Aryan" (306). The stereotype of Jewish effeminacy parallels the stereotype of Jewish intellectuality; both posit that the Jew lacks masculine force.

In *Saving Private Ryan*, the Jew and the intellectual are split apart, "decomposed," in Ernest Jones's terminology. Upham is an intellectual, physically the frailest of the unit, and a coward. Mellish is a capable soldier, a "tough Jew," in Paul Breines's terms, yet the suggestions of homosocial desire that gather around him hint at a hidden effeminacy, and the death he suffers, at the hands of the supremely masculine German soldier, reads as a punishment for that flaw in his masculinity. Upham lives and achieves a kind of manhood, but a manhood that is premised on his renouncing the humane, "intellectual" values he had once stood for. *Saving Private Ryan* ultimately offers an oddly displaced version of a dynamic that Breines, taking his terms from Philip Roth, locates in a good deal of Jewish-American writing in the postwar era, a joining of "saintly Jewish weakness" and "heroic Hebrew force" (22). At the outset Upham embodies the values of humanity and compassion long associated, as Breines points out, with Jewishness, but he is educated through the experience of battle out of this state of bookish naiveté. Upham, as Spielberg's surrogate, undergoes a transformation from gentle to tough, and this transformation is presented not as a regrettable loss of humanity but as a valuable gain in masculinity.

We might look upon Upham's progress as an allegory of Spielberg's own role as movie maker; Spielberg, weirdly, states that Upham is a kind of self-representation: "He was me in the movie....That's how I would have been in war" (qtd. in Schickel 59). Spielberg is surely being ungenerous to himself here. One of the chief conclusions to be drawn from combat memoirs is that there is no way of predicting how one will behave in battle if one has never experienced it; Spielberg might well have surprised himself had he ever been called upon to serve. But Upham most evidently embodies Spielberg's relation, or imagined relation, to the violence that his film represents. Upham exists as an object of identification for Spielberg precisely in order to exorcise the director's anxieties about his authority to tell this particular story. It was a striking aspect of the critical response to the film that *Saving Private Ryan* was able successfully to lay claim to a superior authenticity in its representation of war; reviewer after reviewer, as noted above, insisted that the film had superseded all previous representations of combat, made all other war films "dated and unwatchable" (Hunter B1). There are more than a few World War II movies made by men who either participated in battle (Sam Fuller) or who observed it close-up (John Ford). Yet, this entire body of work was suddenly cast in the shade by *Saving Private Ryan*, relegated to the realm of Hollywood artifice by a movie whose director has never seen combat and who had not yet been born during the historical period in which the film is set.

The film introduces Upham with a certain measure of mockery, a mockery that indicates the uneasiness that Spielberg feels about the authority of his own representations. We are presumably meant to share the skeptical attitude expressed by the battle-hardened members of Miller's platoon toward the book Upham is writing about the "bonds of brotherhood" that develop between soldiers; since Upham has no first-hand experience of combat, his book is presumably empty.[1] In making *Saving Private Ryan*, Spielberg is, of course, in precisely the same position as Upham is in writing his book; he is representing war from a position of second-hand knowledge. The analogy between corporal and filmmaker is reinforced in the scene in which the platoon captures the machine-gun nest; Upham watches the action through a telescope, like a director viewing a scene through the eye-piece of a camera. The distant, abstracted view Upham attains through the telescope, however, is nothing like the

150

vision of hellish turmoil and confusion which we film viewers have been given in the Omaha Beach sequence at the beginning of the film. Upham is an observer, but the way his observation is presented makes us feel, by contrast, like participants; we know, the film assures us, a reality Upham has yet to confront. The film's viewers are encouraged to distance themselves from Upham's naïveté, and so by implication extend to the film the tough, experienced perspective represented by the soldiers.

This is the logic behind the film's structure, much criticized even by some reviewers who responded favorably to the film, in which two heart-pounding battle scenes are bookended around a long and tedious entr'acte. The Omaha Beach sequence makes us feel like veterans, able to share the experienced soldiers' mockery of the naïve Upham. The final battle offers to Upham the experience of warfare that the film has, it implies, already given to its audience. Upham remains – like us – an anguished spectator through the action, but pops up with a rifle at the end, after the outcome of the battle has been decided, to shoot one of the already defeated Germans. Presumably, Upham will go on to write his book, but in a different way, now that he has seen the true face of war. In like fashion, Spielberg's film arrives long after the conflict it depicts has been settled; its contribution to the war effort is as belated and pointless as Upham's. But in representing Upham's transformation, the film argues for its own authority. Because Upham has now learned the dangers of decency and the necessity of savagery, he has acquired the – well, one must call it immoral – authority to write his book. So, Spielberg's movie assures us, because it celebrates cold-blooded murder, it has the authority to represent the experience of war to us. Whatever else Spielberg is, he is the great contemporary master of point of view, a director who knows precisely the way that contradiction can be mobilized to reinforce, rather than undermine, the viewer's engagement with a film and the film's authority for the viewer. Our relation to Upham is compounded of distance and identification. We share the platoon's distance from him as they mock his idealism and ignorance, and we identify with him in his transformation from coward to killer. In the world of Spielberg's cinema, one always has one's cake and eats it too.

Saving Private Ryan has been taken as a cross-generational tribute from the Vietnam generation to the World War II generation, a thank-you note and celebration of what Tom Brokaw has referred to, in the title of his best-selling book, as "The Greatest Generation." Whether this nasty film, with its anti-intellectualism, its devaluing of humanity and compassion, its curious mobilization of anti-semitic stereotypes, is a fitting tribute to the accomplishment of those who fought to defeat fascism, others may decide. But the film's calculated strategies for asserting its own authority to represent the war and displacing previous representations suggest that something more than tribute is going on. The psychoanalyst Harvey Greenberg has argued, with specific reference to Spielberg's *Always*, for the presence of a strain of Oedipal conflict within Spielberg's oeuvre, a generational struggle that operates more in the cinematic than the familial arena, and in which the object of desire is the cultural authority so easily available to the cinema of the war years and so difficult to achieve in the wake of the counterculture. Greenberg's argument is persuasive and helps to explain what is going on in *Saving Private Ryan*, but I confess to finding Spielberg's psyche an uninteresting object of investigation. More urgent, it seems to me, is the task of evaluating the response to the film. Spielberg succeeded in wresting away the authority of the World War II generation to define its own experience, at least in the eyes of reviewers, because of his willingness to press to the limit a seemingly contradictory set of qualities. In its view of motherhood and military command, the film is more sentimental than any World War II film made when that conflict was a living memory could have allowed itself to be. However, in the transformation of Corporal Upham and the connections the film draws between authority, masculinity, and violence, *Saving Private Ryan* is also nastier and more brutish than any previous World War II film. Spielberg hungers after the cultural authority movies possessed in the war years, when Hollywood was conscripted directly into the war effort, but ultimately the only way he has to achieve a similar authority in our disenchanted moment is to deliver a moral consistent with the basest cynicism of our times: humanity is for losers. Surely the generation that helped defeat fascism deserves a better tribute.

Note

1. It is hard to know whether it is more ironic or absurd that, two years after the release of *Saving Private Ryan*, Spielberg (along with the film's star, Tom Hanks) served as executive producer of an HBO miniseries about a group of soldiers in World War II, entitled *Band of Brothers* (2001).

Works Cited

Ansen, David. "Witnessing the Inferno." *Newsweek* 27 July 1998:57.

Bowman, James. "Saving Private Lolita." *American Spectator* September 1998: 68-69.

Breines, Paul. *Tough Jews: Political Fantasies and the Moral Dilemma of American Jewry*. New York: Basic Books, 1990.

Brokaw, Tom. *The Greatest Generation*. New York: Random House, 1998.

Caldwell, Christopher. "Speilberg at War." *Commentary* October 1998: 48-51.

Carson, Tom. "And the Leni Riefenstahl Award for Rapid Nationalism Goes To..." *Esquire* 131.3 (1999): 70, 72, 74-75.

Doherty, Thomas. "*Saving Private Ryan*." *Cinéaste* 24.1 (1998): 68-71.

Gilman, Sander L. *Smart Jews: The Construction of the Image of Jewish Superior Intelligence*. Lincoln: U of Nebraska P, 1996.

Greenberg, Harvey. "Raiders of the Lost Text: Remaking as Contested Homage in *Always*." *Play It Again, Sam: Retakes on Remakes*. Eds. Andrew Horton and Stuart McDougal. Berkeley: U of California P, 1998.

Hunter, Stephen. "Shrouds of Glory." *Washington Poet* 24 July 1998: B1, B5.

Jones, Ernest. *Hamlet and Oedipus*. London: Gollancz, 1949.

Lane, Anthony. "Soldiering On." *New Yorker* 3 August 1998: 77-79.

Menand, Louis. "Jerry Don't Surf." *New York Review of Books* 24 September 1998: 7-8.

Schickel, Richard. "Reel War." *Time* 27 July 1998: 56-59.

Simon, John. "The Best, or the Biggest?" *National Review* 17 August 1998: 51-52.

Weininger, Otto. *Sex and Character*. Trans. Anonymous. London: Heinemann, 1906.

www.ingramcontent.com/pod-product-compliance
Lightning Source LLC
Chambersburg PA
CBHW021332090426
42742CB00008B/580